Harsh Advice for the Unemployed Guy

ASIN: B083XVF8X4

Harsh Advice for the Unemployed Guy

Tough talk to help unemployed young men achieve great success.

By Shepard Humphries

Voluntary Publishing House
Jackson Hole, Wyoming

Free supplemental resources

https://shepardhumphries.com/harsh-resources

Table of Contents

Acknowledgments

There are a lot of individuals who have made my life richer! Society is owed no debt of gratitude, but many individuals are. More on this in the *giving back* portion of the section on 'not falling for crap.'

So, first and most importantly, I want to thank Lynn Sherwood-Humphries, my wife. She is way smarter than I am. She works harder, is more patient, has more self-discipline, and is a motivational gym rat, grandma and intellectually consistent person with many values and morals I respect. Oh yeah, and she is smokin' hot.

While we are on the topic of awesome women, a huge thanks to my longtime loyal friend, employee, partner and editor Ashleigh Read. She, joined by her Oxford commas, (this is when you take a piece of prose, and toss in 10,000 random commas) helped make this book, readable. Any errors you find are suggestions that Asheigh made that I refused to change. Please point them out to me.

Thanks to the jerks, friends, bosses, mentors, and all of the folks that are consistently in my corner. Tony paid me the first dollar I ever earned from writing; thanks Tony. A am fortunate to have a ridiculously large number of friends, and the top 50 are some pretty incredible human beings.

A huge thanks to all of the people that suck in a bunch of ways; they are actually my real motivation. My life, and my grandkid's lives, will be much richer if more people suck less, at least in some ways (...which is why I'm writing this book).

Thanks to my author pal James Joseph; any parts of this book that are well-organized or make sense are because of him. If you think the cover color sucks, or I say stupid stuff, am poorly organized, or you don't like the font, James probably advised me the other way and I ignored him because after all, "He is no Shepard Humphries."

A big thanks to Jeff Bezos, without him and his "I, Pencil" effect, this book would not be in your hands. I hope he remains fabulously wealthy.

Introduction.

I have been poor, "underprivileged," and have worked my way out of a life that was headed nowhere to a successful and good life. I see many young men that are in need of direction, just as I was. Many young men have not had a strong, intelligent and successful male guide in their life. I didn't have a dad present during my youth, perhaps you didn't either. I can't replace our lack of a dad for the last 20 years, but let's give it a shot to overcome this little obstacle, shall we?

I wrote this book for poor men that lack direction, need stronger character, and also lack knowledge and life skills. This book will help them help themselves to become more stoic and successful in finances, relationships, reputation and life in general. I offer this book because 95% of the young men I have encountered recently make me dread the future world my grandchildren will live in. You can be better.

I am a nice guy, but this short book is not about being cordial. When I was 18 years old, a couple mentors sat with me at Bubba's BBQ in Jackson Hole, Wyoming and said a bunch of true stuff. It hurt and I cried. My life was headed nowhere good. I needed to get off my butt, get direction, and design a life worth living. I put my big-boy gloves on and got to it.

Now, almost 30 years later, I am a happily married entrepreneur, grandfather, expert in a couple areas, and have some dollars. I am offering you some advice in a similar style that I received at Bubbas booth #8 so many years ago.

I am going to add some tidbits about things that took me years to learn, things that every man should know, but that few learn until they are old, if even then. Many of my successful middle-aged and old friends "wish I had known at age 25 what I know now." In this book, I will offer many small nuggets that the smartest 20% of readers will actually do something with.

What will you do with what I have to tell you?

It is up to you. I am releasing this book in April of 2020, a time when governments around the world are making it difficult and illegal to be productive. They are doing this as part of their response to a virus named COVID-19. It is a probability that my primary business will be down by 80% or more this year because of their response, and I had a back-up plan. Did you?

The things we discuss in this book will help not only the wayward young man, but the middle-aged and older man that finds himself cast into the financial ruin caused by government action. We can survive if we have the tools.

Shepard Humphries

Section I

What's the Problem?

There are many "producers" that desperately need workers to be on their team, but the only people that seem to apply for the positions are people that want to be an "employee." Still, able bodied people roam our planet claiming, "I can't find a job." What do I mean when I talk about an employee versus a worker versus a job?

Am I complaining that some people want to be employees? 80% of employees have what entrepreneurs call an "employee mindset." This is the kind of person that punches the time clock 1 minute early and leaves right at quitting time. This is the person that exchanges time for money rather than excellence for money. I used to be that kind of person, and now I realize how little value I offered in the free market. Years later I learned that one can still be an "employee" while having an attitude of excellence. Too many people have not yet learned what I did.

Before I get too fired up, let me clarify. If you have a mommy or daddy that has your financial future fully funded, or if Grandmother Ayahuasca told you that materialism is bad and that you will be happier as a minimalist in Thailand smoking weed, great! You just might be onto something. Really—that could be a better path for you; I don't know.

This book is for the person that does not have as much money as he wants, does not have the career he wants, or is working a crappy job and would prefer to be in one of the non-E quadrants. (Learn more later)

Yeah, I included "guy" in the title, and I am speaking primarily to young, unemployed or crappily-employed men. Maybe it is the "privileged cis white male" part of me that made me specify a gender; dunno. Perhaps it's because, as a man, I am able to relate to men and offer relevant experience.

Anyway, this book is good for womenfolk as well as menfolk, and if you haven't picked up on it already, don't expect political correctness: please know that I say a bunch of stuff "tongue in cheek."

Perceptions

Perceptions matter. The way that humans view the world influences how we react to things. Know that you have control not only of how you build yourself to be perceived, but also how you choose to perceive things.

We get to choose how we perceive things in life. We can see a glass of milk as half-empty or half-full. Since the COVID-19 panic of spring 2020 struck, perceptions have driven reactions far more than the virus itself. I have allowed myself to see the (likely) 60% to 80% destruction of my current business as a bad thing. I would be well advised to remember Amor Fati ("I love my fate, good or bad").

Stuff that happens happens. You and I can choose how we perceive the stuff. It is easy to see the destruction of the majority of a business as a "bad" thing rather than as an opportunity. Men that were in the buggy whip manufacturing business when automobiles were invented could either perceive their industry as being "destroyed" or they could choose to look for new ways to thrive in a changing world.

Jobs, work, value production

First, I suggest that you change your perception from wanting to claim a "job" to thinking of your efforts as work contributions to a team effort." Work can be fun, rewarding and easy, but those are not the points of it. Work is what humans do to produce things of value.

Know also that a "job" is not a thing; it is a description of a role that a person can have. A job can not be "lost" and it is never "deserved." Bosses don't owe workers anything beyond the agreed-upon terms. Society does not owe anyone anything except not initiating violence against each individual.

If you are looking for a "job" to satisfy the State Unemployment Insurance Welfare requirements of "job-seeking" then you are likely not of the character that most producers need. If this describes you and you are not willing to work hard and go through the mental and physical pain of facing facts and fixing yourself, read no further. You are worthless in the marketplace. Pray for local, state, federal and international governments to speed up the socialization of our planet. Go get a government job.

If you have not produced or traded your labor, skills, knowledge, or something else of value in the last 7 days, YOU are the problem.

4

Money

Let's talk about money: *what is it?* Is it the root of all evil? Of course not - and neither is the love of it. I really like the way that MJ DeMarko described money in his book "Unscripted." Let's think of money as "value vouchers." These "dollars" are little symbols of value.

Value Vouchers (VVs) themselves are not valuable; however, they are ways to get value. If I worry that I might someday get old, and at that point I will go to a nursing home that costs $6,000 value vouchers each month, I can collect a big pile of VVs and hold on to them in case I need them. I can also trade one VV with another person for a bottle of water.

Calculate your net worth. This is how:

A)   Add the actual "If I could sell it on eBay or Craigslist tomorrow, this is what I would actually be paid for it" value of everything you own. This is your gross net worth.

B)   Add up all of the debt that you have.

C)   Subtract B above from A, and this is your real, or "net" financial worth.

An example:

A)

>Ford Pinto would sell for $3,000 on eBay
>25 books for which a bookstore would pay me $1 each.
>Toaster oven, coffee maker, silverware… $15
>Bed $10

Total assets: $3,050

B)

>I owe my uncle $50 that I borrowed last year.
>I owe $1,470 on my Ford Pinto.

Total debt: $1,530

C)

>Subtract $1,530 from $3,050 to get $1,520.

Your net worth: $1,520.

Money is the way that humans communicate value. We should all be very familiar with what money is and how it works. Do some internet searches to learn more; I find that fee.org and mises.org have good information.

>*Human cooperation means that everybody tries to contribute to the improvement of human conditions. It is in the market that I give something in order that you give something. Exchange leads to higher standards of living. Voluntary exchanges create civilization. -Ludwig von Mises*

Greed

Wanting to have a bunch of value - or value vouchers - is not evil. It is an honorable choice. Some dude that has a "greed level" of ten and works hard, and is a moral and honest person, will collect a lot of VVs. The guy next door with a "greed level" of only two but that steals and/or uses government favors to collect a pile of VVs is not as good of a guy.

Some people choose to be greedy in terms of relationships and they work hard to be nice, kind, helpful and likable. They do this with the greedy desire to have many friends. This is good.

Greed is not a bad thing. Both greedy people and those that are not greedy sometimes do bad things like steal, kill, etc. Greed was not the problem; rather, doing *the bad thing* was the problem.

Section II

Areas of Personal Improvement

If you are still reading, I will assume that you truly want to voluntarily exchange value with others and improve yourself.

The things of value that you have to offer are your time, talent, skills, mental and physical elbow grease, personality, etc...

The things of value that producers can offer YOU in exchange, are money, career growth, education in the production of whatever product or service they provide, and a sense of pride in yourself for being a producer.

It is the producer's duty to negotiate as much value as they can while exchanging the least value.

This is exactly what happens in the voluntary exchange between the producer and their clients. Your "duty" is to negotiate as much of the producer's value for as little of your own value as possible. (After negotiations, I suggest you add more value...)

All parties in voluntary transactions ought to go above their agreed upon "duty" in order to compete with others who also want the same exchange. This is why producers offer more than their duty, for example: paid time off, a fun work environment, "free" coffee from their pot, etc.

So, we have established that you want the thing of value that you receive to be "money." ...Who has money? Rich people, everyone else, profitable companies, and governments. Governments only get their money through taxation, which is theft. You have enough self-respect not to accept stolen money in exchange for your work, so let's take that one off of the table.

You need to do business with rich people, everyone else, or successful companies. When I say "rich people" and "everyone else" I don't necessarily mean extremely wealthy, I simply mean folks that have enough money to pay you for your good or service.

Me, Inc.

Where do you fit into the world? I suggest that you consider your lifetime as an enterprise separate from you as an individual. When you are partnered up with someone through marriage or some other form, the two of you will likely form a joint venture enterprise. My wife and I even have a name for ours.

Under your version of "Me, Inc." you will build a reputation, a net worth, a group of people that are in your corner, and there will even be some that don't like you or your enterprise. This is your "parent company."

Me, Inc. should have a mission statement, a set of values, and should live by clear principles. Me, Inc. should definitely have goals.

Personal responsibility

It is YOUR fault that you are where you are today. Don't be a whiner and complain that you were reared by parents that didn't have money and that didn't teach you how to think properly about it. Boo-hoo.

I don't care about how much you have been crapped on by the world, or about how you have focused on giving the world your gift of modern art that nobody appreciates you for, how hard it is to find a job, that you don't have a good education, or anything else. Buck up, buttercup. I choose to grow and improve, and I came up from big-time poverty. Yep, it makes things more challenging, but that is how it is.

As I write today, I am at a convention in Mexico, and a friend that I have known from this convention for many years, Grant Romundt, did a presentation. His presentation this year stemmed from a one hour presentation he and I attended last year at the same conference. The presentation was about Seasteading, a concept funded in part by Peter Theil.

Now, a year after we both attended the talk, Grant is building a factory in Panama that will house one of the world's largest 3D printers. His company, Ocean Builders, will manufacture floating homes to be placed in the ocean. Check out his project "Ocean Builders" on your favorite search engine.

Grant and I both had the same moment of inspiration. Unlike me, he actually did something useful with it. I must take responsibility and accept that Grant will make tens of millions from this venture over the next years, while I will not. Whose fault is it? Mine!

Whether or not it is true, you should take complete personal responsibility for where your life is, be it good or bad. Having a victim mentality will never help you.

Goals

If you have clear goals; you are more likely to be successful. If you write these goals down, you are even more likely to succeed.

Goals must be clear, realistically achievable and challenging.

Clarity is important. "I want to make more money" is not a good goal. It is not clear. If you earned only one penny more than you did last year, would you be happy? Instead, how about: "I will earn more than $30,000 in pre-tax income this year."

Realistically achievable goals seem more "real," and you will work harder toward them. If you have averaged $13,000 a year in income over the last three years, it is not realistically achievable to set the goal, "I will be a multi-billionaire by the end of this year."

Set your goals high enough that you will have to work hard. If your goals can be achieved with 80% effort for 40 hours a week, your goal is too low.

Following are some sample goals to get your brain turning:

1. I will earn 20% more than last year's $21,457 by December 24th of this year.
2. I will lose six pounds this month.

3. I will spend at least 1 hour each week with my girlfriend, while sitting beside her, without any electronic distractions, and encouraging her to talk.

4. I will consume fewer than 15 bottles of beer this week.

5. I will meditate for at least 5 minutes each morning.

6. I will add $200 to my personal emergency fund savings account every month this year.

7. I will read non-fiction material for at least 1 hour every morning.

8. I will pay at least $100 extra dollars toward the principal on my car loan every month so that I will pay it off by _____ and then be able to put that money toward my _____ .

9. I will contact Shepard and offer to write a 500-word guest post for one of his blogs by the end of this month so that I can hone my writing skills, and build my online presence.

10. I will memorize a 100 or more word poem by the end of this week.

11. I will spend at least 5 minutes learning Spanish every day this year.

12. I will do a yoga pose for at least 2 minutes every day.

Clearly, these are only examples. I suggest that you make a set of goals that works for your unique situation. Every 3 months, make a new set of goals.

What to build yourself into

So, as a person who truly wants to work, what can you do to compete with others seeking money from businesses and other producers? Many of the things I will suggest are illegal for producers to ask for or demand from their employees but are, nonetheless, important. Most items on this list apply to both white-collar and blue-collar jobs.

Have a good personality.

People with weird or unfriendly personalities don't get hired. I know YOU think you are normal, but maybe you are not? If you don't smile frequently, if you speak too much, if you don't "get" jokes, if you are perceived as a geek, hillbilly, wacko etc... many employers will not want you. If you are "different duck" and can't hide it, select a workplace that allows you to channel your uniqueness.

You can change what people see. Ask your friends to write down for you the three best aspects of your personality and the three biggest aspects they think you could improve upon. Allow them the excuse of saying that THEY don't have a problem with your personality, *but* that they think others might incorrectly perceive you as being, "A little bit..." this or that. Let them do it anonymously. (Anonymous Google forms are great for this.)

14

Class

Ok, perhaps this sucks, but I need to break something to you in very plain language, something you have already heard me hinting about. There is a class system in the US.

Yep, there is. The US class system is not as clearly defined as India's caste system; however, it exists, as it does all over the world. It is also fluid, though moving "up" is a real challenge.

Years ago my pal Kim Fadiman talked about the New England aristocracy and how most wealthy folks have weekend homes on the ocean where their families spend much of the summer vacationing. He talked about the sharp rocks in the sea where the children would play while they were growing up, and how their feet became toughened up over the years. By their late teens, they all have very tough feet.

Sister goes off to college and meets a nice boy from an Iowa working class family, and as things get more serious in their relationship, he is invited to join her family at their sea cottage for a summer weekend. He walks out into the water, and his feet are getting cut by the rocks, so he wears an old pair of tennis shoes. Guess who stands out like a sore heel? Guess who has been "outed" as not fitting in? Guess who daddy does not think is good enough for his little girl?

15

Those of us who were born inland and poor can't fix our feet, and there are many other things that we can't fix, too. Are you wondering why I say "fix"? *"Those rich people are not any better than me, are they?"* I agree, but they have the money to hire you to do stuff for them and their companies. My example above, was only of one kind of rich demographic; there are many other kinds of wealthy people around the world.

"Class" is an interesting thing, and is hard to precisely define. Imagine a family with a net worth of two million. The family members drive Chevy Berettas, pick their noses and have tattoos. Is this family more or less classy than the family with a net worth of one million that drives a Mercedes, combs their hair and doesn't pick their noses? Class is not an exact science, so I will make generalizations when I use the word, "classy."

People like similar people

> *"We like people who are similar to us. This fact seems to hold true whether the similarity is in the area of opinions, personality traits, background, or life-style."* — Robert B. Cialdini, *Influence: The Psychology of Persuasion*

I don't know why, but human critters generally tend to hang around with people that are like themselves. We generally like people who are like us: "Oh great, you love that sports-ball team too? Let's tailgate!" The more that we sound, look, smell, and otherwise seem similar, the more likely it is that we will be liked.

We know that if we want to have profitable relationships, we need to be appealing to wealthy people and to the decision-makers in profitable companies. We also know that people like people who are similar to themselves. Add these two ideas, and you will appreciate why the next section is important.

Should we be upset? Is it terribly unfair that people judge us? No, of course not! We all judge everything, and it is a good thing. I judge that latte with extra sweetener to be good, and I judge a tattooed dude leaning over a car hood with a bottle of beer in a brown sack not to be classy. Judging is good, it is reasonable to discriminate against stuff we don't like - including pedophiles, lazy people, stinky people, etc. Some are worse than others, but none come to *my* barbeques.

Be clean

Shower every morning before you go out to meet the world. Even if you don't smell yourself or care about how you look, others notice. There is a general "look" about a person that lets the world know if they showered that morning. My wife describes it as "looking like you care."

If you are overweight, as I have been at various times in my life, you likely produce an odor that is perceived as "unfavorable" by fit folks. They can smell the grease from all of the super-size fries oozing from your pores. You don't smell it because you are with yourself all of the time and are used to it. Other people smell it. Until you lose the fat, you will have to bathe really well and more frequently than fit vegetarians.

Cut your dang hair

Make your hair look like you give a darn. This should be important to a man. I am not suggesting that one must take unreasonable amounts of time to primp like he is getting ready for a metrosexual talent contest, but there are some basics that should always be adhered to. These should be followed until your net worth is equivalent to 1,000 otz of gold.

Your haircut should be conservative, short, & professional. Please notice that I ended the last sentence with a period. Your hair should not be an unnatural color, and it should not be styled and gelled to look European (or, in other words, slept-in and unkempt). The actors in Hollywood can afford to be creative and "express themselves" through silly hairdos, but you cannot until you have your 1,000 otz.

Shave your face

Do not step out of your own home or receive guests unless your facial hair is well groomed. This means that if you can't grow a full beard or mustache, do not let anyone see those scraggly tufts of hair. A patch on your cheek, another patch on your throat… Really, you don't want to present a better version of yourself to the world?

It does not make you less of a man to be unable to grow facial hair, but if you try when you can't, you just look like crap. If you are a red-head like me and your facial hair is sparse or patchy, please stop embarrassing yourself and shave it all off every morning.

A used electric razor can be found at a thrift store for less than $10, and replacement blades can be found for less than $30. Even if you can't afford it, do it anyway or you will never be able to afford other stuff either.

Neck hair matters too. There should be a clear and distinct line between your hair and your bare skin. There is an annoying fuzz that grows, and the great news is that you can shave it off every few days. Really, shave your face every morning! Always! Shave your neck at least every week. Yes, employers notice this stuff.

Clothing

Wear conservative, traditional, clean and pressed clothing. Never wear shorts to a job interview or 'on-the-job' unless and until the employer suggests it.

Wear a button-up shirt to your interview, not a t-shirt. If you must wear a t-shirt, keep it classy. You should be able to wear your favorite T-shirts for a week, and I should not know what your favorite beer is, your favorite cartoon, your favorite rock band, or any information 'promoted' on other swag t-shirts.

I shop at thrift stores in rich towns. Yes, I park my BMW 750li outside, and go in and look for inexpensive stuff. I would not dream of spending $70 for a button-up shirt, and the good news is that some dude up to his ears in debt made that purchase for me, wore the shirt a few times, then donated it. Now, for $5, I get to have a "classy" shirt. I once heard someone tell me that they were broke and therefore couldn't have nice clothes. BS.

Crooked teeth

People with money send their kids to an orthodontist to have their teeth straightened. I got lucky; my mom knew how important teeth are in terms of class, so she found an orthodontist in Cookeville, Tennessee, and explained that we were dirt poor and that she knew how important good teeth are for a person's success in life. She negotiated a barter. She hand-quilted a custom quilt and pillow-cases for

20

the doc and his wife. She put hundreds of hours into that quilt, and a couple years later, our net worth remained at less than $500, but I had classy teeth. I was lucky to have her as my mom.

So, your momma didn't do that for you, and now you are of productive working age, let's say over 14? You will not be hired for jobs dealing with classy people until your teeth are fixed. Sorry. Well, if your employer is desperate, and you have a bunch of other awesome qualities going for you, maybe...

So, I know five thousand bucks or whatever it is is a bunch of money, and you can't afford it right now. Start saving. When you have a couple thousand saved up, check into prices in surrounding countries that have more economic freedom than the US, *intiendo?* You will get more bang for your buck, though this will be easier if you live in San Diego than Birmingham.

You might also check into Invisalign and/or whatever the next version to come on the market might be.

Smart phones

Do not text message, answer your cell phone, or even look at it while in view of your employer or their clients, vendors or others. It is not cool to play games or mess with social media on your boss's dime, even if she "never knows." She knows! Don't be a "typical millennial that is always on his device." Think of your cell phone like farting or picking your nose: don't do it where others can see.

Care, or go away

Care about your service or product—and show your excitement. If you can't make yourself give a darn, go away.

How many clerks have you heard say that they are glad that they are almost done for the day. These whiners should be showing excitement that they *get* to help a great producer provide a great service or great products to great clients. When you ask them how they are, they respond with, "Well, I only have 3 more hours, so I am glad about that." *Losers!* Stick with me here.

Never grumble about long hours, being tired, your personal problems, etc. This is for your friend's or therapist's ears, not for the ears of anyone in the workplace. If you are a clerk at a store, and someone is kind enough to exchange pleasantries, include something positive. "I am excellent, I get to hang out with you for a few minutes. Thanks for being nice and making my day great!"

If you are producing value, you *should* be proud! A hard-working hotel housekeeper is of much higher-value than a non-productive person with a fancy degree. There is great honor in producing value!

Whatever your "thing" is at the time, be passionate about it! If you work at a fast food restaurant in a "menial" position, good for you for being a productive member of society. Having said this, make yourself worth more and get a next-level job doing something that is good for your customers, pays better, and is much more difficult and intellectually stimulating.

How do you get out of the fast-food joint? Be the best burger-flipper that they have ever had, and donate an extra hour a day to the place, making it better and learning new aspects of the industry.

Read the policy manual repeatedly and see if you can discover what is important to employers and important for profit... If the book says not to pick your nose and put your boogers in the shake machine, know that someone once did that, and that's why the policy exists. Read about all the other stuff, and you will have a great idea of what is actually needed for a business to be successful.

If you work at a fast-food place selling chemical-laden high-carb food that is poisoning people, you should not feel proud about the food products that you sell, but you should feel pride about what you are doing for the company. Your "products" are your skilled labor and contagiously positive attitude. You can be proud of the service you provide!

Be a ray of sunlight to your co-workers; challenge them to be awesome; mentor them without them even knowing it. *"Hey man, I bet I can up-sell more milkshakes in the next hour than you."*

Be in good physical condition

If you are chubby or fat, this shows that you have a lack of personal discipline in diet and that you "don't care" enough to invest 20 minutes a day (4% of the minutes in a day) jumping rope in your living room or back yard. Get yourself into average or better condition.

You can safely lose 2 pounds per week by diet alone. Boost this with a weekly 48-hour water-only fast. Don't work out on these days; you won't have the energy. If you are truly overweight, get some good advice from someone that knows more than me. I asked my pal Greg Papanicolas for some quick-start advice.

24

People often overlook bodyweight training because they think it's not hard enough. But it's certainly possible to build muscle using only your own bodyweight, especially if you can turn it into a challenge.

You start each set with an isometric hold at a key position in the movement. What does this mean? If you're after muscle growth, use the position where you can feel the most tension in the target muscle. Hold a squat at the mid way point for 10-60 and hold a pushup from the same mid way point for 5-30 seconds. Do a couple of sets of this.

This is called isometric training and it will fatigue the muscle to the point where you won't even have to leave your house to get a great workout in. If you are curious about more unique exercises you can add to your home routine, or if you want more information about general fitness, you can find me, Greg Papanicolas, at projectspartacoaching.com

Be certain that you have a high enough level of health and the stamina to get the job done. By getting into great shape, you will have more energy to achieve your goals.

Injuries

Do you have a bad ankle or back or neck? Tell your prospective employer in writing that *this is your problem, not theirs*. Let them know that it is a preexisting injury and that you intend to work around the pain and NOT claim worker's comp and thereby raise the employer's rates with the government. (Yes, that really is the way it works.)

Same thing goes for "unemployment welfare." Let your employer know that you have too much pride to accept welfare through the government's unemployment insurance welfare program. Be honest. They are not allowed to ask you to do this, but they will appreciate hearing your attitude.

Have a good work ethic

While learning the new business, plan to study or practice the skills on your own time without pay. After that, plan to start work 15 minutes to one hour early every day and not ask to be paid for it. Plan to work hard all day long. Plan to stay after quitting time without pay in order to get the job done.

Learn the duties (on your own time) of others at your workplace. Perhaps if you are a janitor, you could help the bookkeeper with filing? Learn about all aspects of the business with excitement. Pick up at least three pieces of

26

trash every day at your job-site, especially when no one is watching.

The US government came up with an arbitrary number of hours that constitute a "workweek." Are you ready for the real-world truth? **40 hours is not enough time to get stuff done**. Most self-employed people work at least 60 hours, and many work over 90 hours a week.

Many employers cannot afford to pay you time and a half to work beyond 40 hours, but you should try to sneak behind the government's back to produce at least 50 hours every week, even though you are only paid for 40. This is not legal for employers to ask of you, but people that do this are not unemployed ... savvy?

Focus

Be focused. You can not do twelve different projects well. Prioritize the top one, two, or three. Once those projects are done, you can add more. This is a constant challenge for me, so please learn from my warning about my problems and do not repeat them. It is amazing how quickly a project can be completed when my focus is intense. When I interrupt my progress by doing a dozen other things, none of them get done.

Be appropriate

Until you have your first million bucks in the bank, be appropriate. Don't make offensive comments, even if *you* think they are funny. People are listening, both in person and on social media. They will not contact you and tell you that they were offended by something; however, they are less likely to hire or recommend you to someone else.

Don't have a romantic relationship with anyone where you work. In some cases, it will seem appropriate, and if that is the case, I have some advice for you: DON'T have a romantic relationship with anyone where you work.

No foul language

Take the F-word out of your vocabulary for the next year. This goes for your Facebook page as well. The person "of means" that could exchange great value with you probably doesn't like hearing a potty mouth, and even if they do, some of the people they might introduce you to won't like hearing it.

I know that it might have been normal when you were shooting our neighbors over in the sandbox, working in the kitchen at the greasy spoon or in the lube shop. Nobody will miss your potty mouth. Stop. Even if everyone around you is using naughty words, you should not. It will pay off in the years to come.

Friends

"We become the average of the 5 people we spend the most time with." -Jim Rohn

Who are YOUR friends? Does your relationship with them make your life richer? Do you add value to each other's lives? Do you do positive things with each other when you are together? Do you discuss big ideas? Are you honest and kind and blunt and optimistic with each other?

I have dumped friends and I have purposefully let other folks gently drift further away. Seasons of life change, and this is OK. Don't let losers drag you down. Cultivate friendships that make you better.

Friendships and connections can also become one of your greatest assets. The more high-quality people that you meet and get to know, the more opportunities you will have. Your character, talents and reputation are very important.

When times are tough and the job market is a challenge, or starting a new business is not as easy as you had hoped, think about how much more appealing a "known entity" is to an employer or customer. A contractor is more likely to hire a laborer friend than a laborer stranger. Potential clients are more likely to do business with someone they know, like, and trust. It's all about who you know, you know?

Stoicism

I have mentioned being stoic; what does that mean?

Back about 2,300 years before the Internet, in Athens Greece, some smart folks came up with this way of thinking. It is based on logic and reason and is a way of figuring out the world around us and living well in that world. Stoics believed that virtue, the highest good, is based on knowledge; the wise live in harmony with the natural state of things. They believed that humans should be solid and steadfast, not making a big deal out of fortune, poverty, pleasure or pain.

Stoic advice is incorporated throughout this book, and I suggest that you take a few minutes each day to look up a quote on stoicism and contemplate it. The four primary virtues are wisdom, morality, courage, and moderation.

Let's contemplate a handful of stoic quotes to get started.

> *"Work done for a reward is much lower than work done in the Yoga of wisdom. Set thy heart upon thy work, but never on its reward. Work not for the reward; but never cease to do thy work." —The Bhagavad Gita*

> *A gem cannot be polished without friction, nor a man perfected without trials. -Seneca*

Failure and deprivation are the best educators and purifiers. -Albert Einstein

He has the most who is content with the least. -Diogenes

The first rule is to keep an untroubled spirit. The second is to look things in the face and know them for what they are. -Marcus Aurelius

Don't explain your philosophy. Embody it. -Epictetus

It would also be wonderful use of your time to watch some videos or read books by Ryan Holiday of the Daily Stoic.

Be on time

"If you are not 10 minutes early; you are late."
-Vince Lombardi

Do not create extra work for your employer. Life happens: kids get sick, great snow lands on the mountain, cars break down, alarms mess up, etc... *People who have and keep great jobs are always at work when they are scheduled to be.* Always.

This is part of being a man of your word. No excuses. If someone is ever late to a meeting with me, they can kiss the opportunity goodbye. As a matter of fact, three minutes before a meeting is scheduled to begin, if the person has not arrived, I start packing up my laptop or notebook and at one minute after the scheduled meeting time, I leave.

Yeah, I know traffic was heavy. I know you stopped to help a lady change her tire. I know it was tough to find parking.

(OK, so the lady with the tire. Think about this scenario and about the meeting. If you are meeting a pal for coffee, maybe send a text letting her know you will be 15 minutes late because you are helping someone with a flat tire. If the meeting was for a job interview? Unless the gal is in danger, is it best to help someone with something anyone could do for them or to get your financial life on track? That is a personal choice, but don't you ever use your

32

kindness to the lady as an excuse for why *you* are "broke.")

Part of being stoic is thinking ahead and coming up with solutions for potential problems before they happen. Plan to arrive at important meetings 30 minutes early; this will give you the buffer time to help the stranded motorist.

Consider things that you can control, like rear-ending another driver. A great trick is to keep an eye on the brake lights *several vehicles ahead of you* so that you will have more warning. Stay back from the car in front of you by at least two seconds; this will give you time to stop if they slam on their brakes. You can't control their brakes; you can control your distance from them.

Communication

How to speak - Be kind and polite and use clear, direct, and precise language. Speak loudly enough that your audience can hear you. Misunderstandings can result if you avoid the challenge of remembering to speak at a volume and in a style that can be heard.

Be self-aware. Know that when you speak to someone, they must be able to hear and understand you. If they are standing near a noisy thing, or if you are facing away from them, either speak more loudly or simply flip them off to

33

let them know you don't respect them enough to communicate clearly.

Communication is a loop. When I send a message, the loop is not yet complete. You must hear the message and respond. This goes for written, verbal, and other kinds of communication. Yes, text messages also. Respond to the person communicating with you!

Oh yeah, and stop mumbling. Assume that everyone you are speaking to is slightly hard of hearing. Don't yell, but enunciate your words well. Listen to a few videos by Andreas M. Antonopoulos on YouTube. He speaks so clearly that everyone can understand him.

Be straightforward and clear when you speak, however be gentle, polite and respectful. Have difficult conversations, and stay calm with a slight smile on your face as you speak.

How to listen - My friend and mentor Carl Watner is a very precise speaker and is very direct in his tone. His goal in writing and speaking is not to make me feel "special" or worthwhile; he communicates *truth*. Sometimes I write something to him and his response hurts my poor little feelings. It is very much worth it.

I once sent him an outline of a book I was contemplating writing, and Carl's response was something like, "I am disappointed, it is not good at all." He could have said, "It has room for improvement, keep going," and I could have wasted time. Instead, he said what he meant.

Understand that the careless speaker is responsible for the emotions they feel when a precise person "calls them" on a topic. The precise person did not make the careless speaker "feel like an idiot." The speaker chose to use words and speak on topics with which they were not familiar.

Using the word "balloon" when in fact the phrase "internal combustion engine" should have been used, does not make the engineer a jerk when he calls the speaker out on it. Be humble and accept corrections.

If you know more than the person with whom you are speaking, rethink that assumption. Is it really true? Whether or not it is true, you will probably benefit more from doing a lot more listening than speaking.

"If you are the smartest man in the room, you are in the wrong room." -Author unknown

"Wise men speak because they have something to say; Fools because they have to say something." -Plato

Plan to produce

Plan to produce something of value for a minimum of 10 hours a day, whether you have a "job" or not. This can include work-seeking, volunteer work, and educating yourself with the reading list I share and with quality videos.

The point is that you sleep 8 hours, and you eat, poop, shave and shower for another hour, leaving you with 15 hours a day. Heck, take a third of it to relax or have fun. The remaining 10 hours each day belong to YOU Inc. You have a life to build, and 70 hours a week will get you well on your way.

Work for free if necessary, read a book a day, volunteer for a successful business, write articles or books, take photos for small businesses' social media - just stay busy being productive! Are you lacking imagination? Maybe a couple ideas will help get your creative juices flowing:

Cleaner idea

$2.12 buys you paper towels and Glass Cleaner at the Dollar Tree in Jackson, Wyoming. A broom costs $1.06.

Now, go to a place in public view and start cleaning stuff. People will ask you what you are doing, which gives you the opportunity to hand them your resume and tell them that your personal work ethic requires that you work 10 hours a day every day, but that you don't have an employer sponsoring you at the moment.

Have you ever heard of anyone doing something like this? Nope, me neither. You will stand out in the crowd, and opportunities will come your way!

Highway cleanup idea

Set up a large cardboard sign along a highway with letters that are readable at 55 MPH from 300 yards away that says, **"I like to work, but am not employed. Resumé here."** Put a stack of resumes in a plastic bag under a rock by the sign.

Now, walk along the highway (upstream) quickly picking up trash. What better way to demonstrate your work ethic? If you did this every day for 2 weeks during rush hour, what do you think might happen? Yes, this is not something that most unemployed folks do.

Don't have a resume?

Find a libertarian-leaning business owner or other accomplished entrepreneur and respectfully ask them to help you make one. Heck, write to me and I will help you. It should not take more than two to four hours to make a great one.

Don't have a computer or a printer and don't have money for paper? Ask five folks from the above described business-folks if you may use theirs in exchange for sweeping their parking lot.

I bet four of them will say yes. If not, and as a last resort, many governments have libraries that have free computer use allowed.

Consider having several versions of resumes for different people / opportunities. If you are going for a professional book-editing opportunity, your resume will be very different than if you are in TEOTWAWKI (The End of the world as we know it) mode and are trying to convince a rancher to allow you to stay on his ranch for a year and exchange labor for food and shelter. Have several of both kinds of these resumes, along with reference letters/paragraphs, printed out in case you have to bug out and are not able to print things.

Don't nickel and dime

I tested an employee recently, and perhaps two lessons can be learned. For the last couple of weeks a remote employee from another country has been doing small projects for me. One was a $15 gig, and I instead paid her $20, plus the $1 that PayPal charges me.

I mentioned to her that PayPal was expensive for transactions, and that I wanted to bundle more things. She suggested that I tell PayPal that I am giving a gift to friends and family so that it would be free. Well, now I know about her integrity. I now know that for as little as $1 she will lie. I will still hire her for projects, but now there is way less trust.

Then, two days ago, she did a $3 job for me. In less than 20 hours she wrote asking when I was going to pay her. I had a $65 job planned for her the next week, which in her country is more than two days of pay. I sent her her dang $3 and paid the extra $1 to send it. I hired someone else to do the $65 job.

She just cost herself some money in the long run. I will use her services much less. If I need a quick something transcribed, I will simply do it myself. It is likely that by being penny-wise and pound foolish, she will have lost a potential week or two of income over the next year.

Beyond the lessons of integrity and not nickel and diming, consider another important concept: that "stuff averages out". Yes, last month you worked 20 extra hours that you didn't ask or receive payment for. Next month, I bet some really good things will happen to you. It will "average out."

Yes, your trade of labor and skills might not be a direct thing; however, maybe instead of cleaning toilets as your normal task, next week the boss will ask you to take his truck to the neighboring town to pick up some supplies. That is 5 hours of relaxing time to listen to part of a book on Audible, and that is pretty nice. Good things seem to happen to folks who go above and beyond and don't nickel and dime.

By the way, do you think that anyone who has ever done an errand for the boss has ever washed the boss's truck on the way back and not charged for it? Has anyone wiped the dashboard down and made sure the truck was a bit cleaner than when they picked it up? Might that be smart?

Ashleigh, the woman who edited this book, has also worked with me on other projects. Recently, she used her linguist skills to translate our company's summary description into Hebrew. She did not charge for this. She could have charged me 10 or 20 bucks or more for doing it, but she didn't. She lost out, right? No, she just got a plug in a soon-to-be best-selling book about her editing and linguistic talents.

Be a YES man!

It is funniest when my wife says it: she will tell people that the two of us are, "Yes men." We almost always say "yes" and try new things.

If anyone asks you to try something or offers you something, seriously consider doing it! A pal that is a pizza delivery guy sprains his ankle and asks you to cover his shift. Say, "yes!" I would, even at this stage in my life.

I have never delivered pizza, but I would love to have another skill and "experience" in yet another area. I would of course tell the boss that I have never delivered pizza and that I don't feel I deserve to be paid. I would bust my butt, work hard, thrill my clients, mess up, fix it, and have a great time. I promise you that by the end of the shift, I would have a full-time job offer.

Following are some examples of "yeses" I have said over the last year:

Cowboy

Last year some friends who are ranchers asked for help with branding. "Yes!" I had never done this before, however I learned a bunch about the cattle business, got my pants completely soaked with cow crap, and learned to respect my friends even more. They saw my learning curve. I failed, I learned, and I worked hard. They want me to help them with branding again.

Mentoring

My operations manager's girlfriend asked for some mentoring assistance. Recently, we met for 3 hours as I taught her basic website design and SEO. I am now better at mentoring, and I have created great value.

> *By the way, when a mentor helps a mentee, and the mentee actually follows through and does well, the mentor wants to help them even more.*

Cross-marketing

The day before the meeting with my mentee, I reached out to a new business in my town and invited the owner for a latte. His business is a mobile auto-repair service in the wealthiest county in the country. Smart. His wife is a marketing whiz. We are now each writing blog posts on our respective webpages to help promote the other. I bet that we will both go above and beyond. We will both give more value than promised. He said, "Yes."

Car and car transport

I started a business mastermind group a couple of years ago, and one member owns a car dealership. He and his dad own another dealership about 6 hours away in the same town where my dad is in the Alzheimer's Hospital.

Because my pal said "yes" to the mastermind group, and because we have both said a bunch of mutually beneficial "yeses" since then, I typically do a vehicle swap for him when I visit my pa. He pays gas one way, I get no wear and tear on my personal car, and it works out.

A few months ago, he had a nice used BMW 750li that wasn't selling, so he and his sales manager, also a great friend, sold it to me for a wholesale price.

I would not have ever considered a "status" car like that as a prudent option to add to my driveway; however, because of a bunch of "yeses" that did not pay off immediately, we are both "ahead." That car can either be used for driving, or it can be sold to make some mortgage payments.

By saying yes to various opportunities, including the small sample above, my life has been made richer. I know more, have more skills and experience, and am encouraged to keep saying, "yes!"

Fail & learn

 Be willing to fail. This is an important concept, and I have embraced it over the years; I have profited in a big way.

The idea is that you should not wait for everything to be completely perfect before you leap. If you wait to write a book until you "know more," you will wait forever. If you wait to get a job until the "right one" comes along, you will wait a long time. If you keep waiting and making excuses for things, you will never get things done.

Ego can also get in the way. You might be afraid of being embarrassed that you are not good enough. The truth is that, unless they are paying you to do it, nobody really cares about you or how well you do at something.

I quit being a cop and started a security / property caretaking business. Over the course of 10 months, I failed at it in a big way, and I learned a lot.

- I learned that my wife was willing to financially support our household for 10 months while I tried to get things going.
- I learned what kind of security services were not wanted, at least at the price I offered them.
- I learned that spending $17,000 on marketing gave me a return of ZERO, and that the few clients I *did* acquire were all through word of mouth.
- I learned about website building, graphic design, and my DISC profile.
- I learned who was really in my corner and who wasn't.
- I learned how my competitors marketed their businesses.
- I increased my "market research" skills.
- I learned about dozens of other aspects of the minutiae of being a small business owner.

All of these failures were incredible! They were WAY better than an associate degree in business. Even if you don't want to be an entrepreneur, I suggest that you start a small business with full expectations that it is unlikely to succeed. You will learn SO much!

Try stuff and fail and learn and try something else. I have given several examples in this book of things I have tried and failed. This is a big deal: do it! Fail & learn!

> As a side note, some say that, "Trying is all that matters." I call BS. If I ask you to do a thing for me and you try really hard and fail, you have been worthless to me. YOU might have benefited from learning a lesson, however as far as I am concerned, you failed. Don't you dare ever say to a boss, "Sorry, I tried."

> You just failed your boss, so an apology is perhaps in order, though an apology is basically just you sharing your emotion of remorse with someone. Wait, you just failed your boss, and now you want her to listen to you pour out your emotions without paying her therapist's fees? She doesn't care if you are experiencing the emotion of feeling "really sorry." And now you are going to negate any actual sincerity of your apology and explain away your failure and your apology by saying, "At least I tried?" Knock it off and grow a pair. All she wants

is for you to learn from it, never make that or similar mistakes again, and make it right.

Does it sound like I am speaking out of both sides of my mouth here? First I tell you to try and fail, then I say that your failures are useless to other people, as are your "tries." YOU benefit from failures, but other people do not, at least in the short term.

If I ask you to dig a hole, and you tell me that you have never done that work before, and you agree to do the work but will not charge me while you are in the learning / failure stage, I will respect you, hire you, and be patient.

If on the other hand I ask you to do it and you say yes, you charge me full price and excuse your failure away by telling me that you tried, well, you just failed again.

"Remember that failure is an event, not a person." -Zig Ziglar

47

Decide what quadrant you prefer

I'm about to teach you some learnin' from the book Cash Flow Quadrant by Robert Kioysaki. This book is on your reading list, and you will learn more when you read it; however, I will give a brief summary here.

There are four basic categories that we can get value vouchers from. "E" is for employee. This is a person that does a task and is paid for their time. This includes burger flippers, hotel clerks, presidents of companies, NFL coaches, janitors, teachers, and cops. Most people fall into this category. They don't mind being told what to do, and they are afraid of risk.

"S" is for self-employed. This is when you own your job. A dentist who owns his dental office is an "S," and so are most small business owners. Bill of "Bill's Plumbing" is probably an "S." A few "S" owners are able to grow their enterprise into an actual "B," a business.

A "B" is when the business can function without the owner. If Bill the plumber hires people to handle all aspects of his business, and he is able to sit on the balcony in an eighth floor room at the Hotel Emperio in Acapulco at nine in the morning on a Monday listening to waves crash while writing a book, he is in the "B" category. (Yes, that is where I am writing from this morning)

48

The "B" category is challenging, especially for small businesses. It is possible that the managers and other people in the systems that make Bill's and my businesses run could be in a car crash today. Guess who has to take over and make stuff work? Yep, Bill and I have to. This means we are not truly "all the way there" in terms of the "B" quadrant.

Many of us hope to get into the I quadrant. I stands for Investor, and this is pretty ideal as you will learn when you read the book.

In which quadrant are you most comfortable, by nature? In which quadrant do you want to be in five years? What about in ten years?

Bootstrapping a business

In almost every case, this is the best way to start a business. Bootstrapping means that you don't borrow money from outsiders, and instead you scratch and claw and get creative. In this way, you will own 100% of the business in the end.

The challenge with crowdfunding or borrowing money is that you learn less and feel less pain. Pain is important because it helps us grow. Your first three businesses are likely to flop, and you do not want to let your friends, family, or banker down.

I almost always turn down funding requests from friends who are starting their first business. Their plan, understanding of business, and other factors would have to be incredibly impressive to overcome this hurdle. I want them to have to grind and learn many important lessons that extra money can hide.

Learn skills and get talented

Think about all of the things that you could learn and master to be of more value to others. As a matter of fact, even if you do not reach mastery, learning more than most is always of value.

Scott Adams coined the term, "Talent Stack." I like it. In essence, the idea is that the more things that we can become talented in, the better. Even if you make a good living as a typist, you will be a more valuable human if you also know how to do carpentry, change an oil filter, edit a book, etc.

Growing your talents in many areas is almost like having your foot in the door of many fields of expertise. It is wise to diversify your talents beyond things similar to your main expertise. In other words, if you are a website builder, be sure to also learn some physical skills in auto repair, home construction, farming, etc. If the world remains safe, secure, and unchanging, you might never need these skills.

If, on the other hand, things change (as they always have), computers could be useless. People might think that having their refrigerator fixed is more important than having a new logo designed. It is better to have a talent stack that includes graphic design, website development, refrigerator repair, and shoe repair than to have one that only includes graphic design and website design.

Imagine being "better than 95% of people" at shoe repair, website design, splinter removal, spelling, marketing, branding of calves, and food preparation. Imagine having another two dozen skills and talents. See Appendix 2 for a longer list.

Mr. Adams makes another excellent point about stacking these talents. There might be 100 other people in your community that know how to prepare food in a safe way; however, do they also know how to do website design? If you can stack several of your talents on top of each other, you become even more unique and needed.

For example, of the thousand people that live in my subdivision in Jackson Wyoming, I estimate to be better than 990 of them at:

- Firearms Training
- Logic
- Teaching
- Customer service training
- Leather repair
- Interview & Interrogation
- Taxidermy
- Book publishing
- Executive protection
- Long range shooting
- Website design
- Creative Marketing
- Intellectual honesty
- Pistol shooting
- Propaganda & Public Relations
- Philosophy of Voluntaryism
- Austrian economics
- Video editing
- Debunking conspiracy theories
- Knowledge of sales strategy
- Neuro Linguistic Programing
- Leadership

Not all of these are marketable talents; however, they can bring richness and understanding to life. Imagine stacking three of these talents. Assemble the ten best people from my subdivision in terms of ability to design a website. How many of those people also have my level of expertise in video editing? Maybe 3. By the time we get to the third talent of Austrian Economics, none of those three have my knowledge, or have likely even heard of the Austrian School. So, is this particular stack of three talents marketable? Dunno.

Recently, my mother-in-law Judy had a flat tire on her travel van. It had been many years since I had changed a tire, so I went to her house and re-familiarized myself with a basic skill every man should know.

Having multiple talents, skills and diverse knowledge will greatly improve your life, and it can also bring you your lowest moments. If I had not studied propaganda and voluntaryism, and if I were not knowledgeable in macroeconomics, observing governments "doing their thing" would not bug me as much. Ignorance is bliss, and 995 people in my subdivision probably choose it. As with the cashflow quadrant, you might be happier in an "easier" place.

> *"It is the mark of a truly educated man to know what not to read." — Ezra Taft Benson*

Care

Care about not only *your* work performance, but the performance of the company. If the company excels, so do you. If it fails, guess what. So do you.

Even when you are not officially working, think about ways you can increase business and help market your employer's business.

Tell everyone you know what a great place to work your place is, that the bosses are awesome, and that the product or service you provide is awesome. "Ride for the brand" and give a darn. If you don't care about what it is that you are doing, leave. You are a drain on the company and it is a drain on you.

Be frugal

Now is not the time in your life to blow money on cigarettes, downloading movies, lottery tickets etc.

> *"Never live at the level that matches your income. Your standard of living, instead, should match your next-best employment opportunity, the one you have forgone or the one you might take next. If you stick with this practice—it requires discipline—you will be free to choose where you work and to take*

greater risks. You will also develop a cushion should something go wrong." -Jeffrey A. Tucker

Spend at least the next 6 months being a tightwad. Many smart folks remain frugal their whole lives. I recall a wealthy woman in Muddy Pond where I was reared; she said that people asked her why she would cut her worn-out bedsheets in half and then sew the unworn sides in the middle to get more use.

> Poor people: "You have a lot of money, why do you do that?"

> Rich woman: "Doing things like that is the reason I have money."

Don't buy cheap new cars, rather, buy older cars with low miles and high quality. Nothing says "low class" like an inexpensive American-made car with accessories on it. I know the people in the mobile home park think that the spoiler on your brand new Dodge Dart looks way better with the reclining hot-body gal sticker on it, but people with a net worth over 1000 otz. are rolling their eyes in sadness and have pegged you as a loser.

Tattoos & piercings

Don't even think of getting a tattoo until your net worth is over a 1000 otz. of gold. My rule is that you allow yourself one tattoo for every 1000 otz. of net worth you acquire.

Tattoos are perceived by most successful people as a low-class thing. If you think they are cool, enjoy them on other people, but don't mess your own body up. Either hide your tattoos beneath clothing, or have them removed.

Some exceptions include: if you are getting too many job offers, wealthy women keep checking you out and you wish they would just go away, or if you are lonely and feel that cops do not pay enough attention to you. If this is your situation, get tattoos so that cops will pay more attention to you and employers won't. Chase away women if that is what you want.

I get that everyone else in your former socio-economic group has tattoos, smokes cigarettes, and buys lottery tickets. Please stop doing these things and start reversing the harm already done.

Already have tattoos? If they can be covered 100% of the time by the clothes you wear; great. If they can't, start saving your money to get them removed.

Guess what I think about piercings? OK, one exception, if you are a woman, earrings are OK. Mature, rational and conservative-leaning folks look at the eyebrow spike or nose ring and think, "This poor young man has such low self esteem that he looked in the mirror one morning, hated what he saw, and thought he would look better if he had all manner of metal stuff sticking out of his body. How sad." Yes, that is what "normal" people, the people you want to go into business with, think. Like tattoos, go for it once you have enough value vouchers saved up, just not yet.

> *"You are free to choose, but you are not free to alter the consequences of your decisions."*
> — *Ezra Taft Benson*

Don't have children...yet

Kids are expensive from a time perspective, and also from a financial perspective. 100-hour weeks for ten to 20 years are a pretty good way to "get ahead" financially. Make a choice. Forget "balance" and make a choice. If you already have a child, your choice has been made, and I suggest that you make them the priority.

Children should not be sent to government schools, and probably not even private schools. Period. John Taylor Gatto explains how important this is in his wonderful books. This means that someone needs to be at home with them for at least 14 years, 24/7.

If you are worth a darn as a parent, you will not park your children in front of a TV or other screen; you will be reading with them, playing games, exploring your neighborhood, etc. Does all of this mesh with your professional goals? Do you have time for that joyful project?

As Jordan Petersen brilliantly explains, many childless women in their 30's have a strong urge to have a kiddo. What should you do if your lady wants a child and you don't? Talk about it frankly, and make a decision that you are both OK with, even if this means going your separate ways. I don't suggest you break off otherwise wonderful relationships, but in 10 years, do you really want to resent each other for not having a child or for not being millionaires?

Eat healthy foods

Don't buy low-value food like fast food, candy bars, sodas, cigarettes, weed or such. Yep, I guess I did just call weed a "food." Shows to go you I am illiterate about it.

Really though, each one of your value vouchers can either disappear or can work for you. It is better to buy another $15 Audible book about marketing than to buy three Big Mac meals. Me, Inc. deserves better!

Don't smoke

Cigarettes are expensive and don't help you. They stink. They are currently out of social favor among the mainstream "producer" demographic, and you will be judged for it. I know that you think that if you extend your neck when you exhale loudly; it will keep the stink out of your clothes. That doesn't work.

I, and many other non-smokers, can smell smoke on you regardless of having the window open, etc. Stop smoking. Stop complaining about the addictive substances in cigarettes and quit. It will not be easy. Make it happen.

Did you just mutter, "But Shepard, it is easy for you to say, you don't smoke and don't realize how addictive it is." Really? You want to go there? OK.

No, I didn't make a crappy choice many years ago that led to an addiction. You screwed up starting that junk, and just because "addiction specialists" are excited to make excuses for you doesn't matter outside of your "safe place healing group." Dude, stop it. It will suck, then your life will be better.

Drug use

Nope, not yet. Drugs are expensive, and they take you out of the reality that you need to exist in in order to thrive. You *are* allowed to consider taking a single dose of a psychedelic "medicine." I urge you to wait though, until you have tripled your current net worth. Using this "creativity-boosting" drug is only prudent if you lack inspiration and are willing to take the risk to possibly acquire some new ideas. My advice to abstain from drugs applies to both the kind that the government likes and the kind they don't like.

Alcohol: the truth serum

"He is a mean drunk." "She turns into a slut when she gets drunk." "He has a temper problem when he drinks."

Bullcrap. We all are who we are. Alcohol enhances our true selves; it does not change us. Do you have a tendency to get into fights when you go bar-hopping? You are a jerk. Stop drinking so that you don't ruin your life. If you tend to be funny, relaxed, and more understanding and loving when you drink, go for it. You get to choose what you do; does drinking alcohol serve you well? Overindulgence can be very harmful, not just hurting your ability to show up ready to work hard the next morning, but in terms of public perception as well.

Wait, what about the expense of drinking? Add up what you spend each month and multiply that by 12 months. During one period of my adult life, I enjoyed about $12 worth of alcohol every night. I don't know what 365 days of a daily expense of $12 is, but it is probably a good amount of value vouchers. Yeah, couldn't you invest that elsewhere?

It occurs to me that alcohol is like the other drugs, better to skip it for now.

Don't waste your time in jail

So, how does one stay out of jail? This might crimp your style some, but these simple things will give you a 99% chance of not being put in jail.

1. Don't drink alcohol heavily.
2. If you have had more than one average-sized drink, don't drive.
3. Don't initiate violence against people or property.
4. Don't steal or defraud anyone.
5. Don't use or sell cannabis, even if your local state government allows it. At the time of printing, the federal government still considers THC a criminal thing. Definitely don't use or sell the "harder stuff."
6. If you have been accused more than once of threatening a woman, being scary, being late on child support payments, stalking, harassing women,

or hitting or abusing women; stop having romantic relationships.

Why do I suggest such a drastic thing like not having romantic relationships? Because if you've had multiple complaints, you're headed in a bad direction, and when stuff inevitably goes really wrong, it will destroy your life. Wait, what? You heard me. You are probably the problem. The market has spoken. You are not the victim over and over and over. I know that you don't think that you are the problem, but you are. This is an opportunity for you to practice being a better thinker and planner of your destiny.

I have never been accused of stalking, emotional abuse, physical abuse, being a deadbeat dad, harassment or anything like that. 95% of men also have not had anyone waving red flags. Yes, occasionally a guy that is completely innocent is attacked by the she-woman man haters, but it is rare. For it to happen two or three or eight times? Come on.

So, let's assume that you are a mean person when you get drunk. You stick out your lower jaw and scowl in an intimidating way toward your wife or girlfriend. You have a personality type that needs work. I don't dislike you, but you are being a jerk. Let's hang out more so you can watch me and the people I surround myself with treat everyone with respect. I want you to be better.

If you are dating and you have "issues" as highlighted by past folks you have dated, take a year off from dating and fix yourself, then try again. Why do I suggest such dramatic action? The consequences can be huge. In today's society, the standard operating procedure for the system is to turn female victims of mean men into lifelong victims who attend therapy. Your actions, and the mainstream response, helps these women's lives be ruined. Don't be a part of it.

Yeah, I know some people get lonely. It will suck not having a romantic partner for a year. Oh well, toughen up buttercup. Get to work on building your life and the important social and business relationships we discussed earlier. Build yourself into the kind of man that all women will want and that your daughter would deserve. Step up, man.

You do not want a restraining order, a conviction for family violence or stalking etc. You don't want to be on the black list at the local cop shop. You don't want to be sentenced to mandatory anger management schooling in the middle of your workday so that you get fired.

So, you have a list of only six things that will keep you out of an expensive and messed up jail system. It is simple.

The only exception would be your principles. If a law says that you have to report where the neighbor Jew or Muslim dude is hiding so that he can be captured can be put on a cattle car, you might choose to give up your freedom and

63

maybe your "life" for your principles. Otherwise, don't go to jail for white-trashy preventable reasons.

In the "Don't Fall for Crap" section, we will discuss the jail industry, and add some reasons why you should stay away.

Keep work life separate from personal life.

Leave family affairs, kid or wife troubles, or anything that doesn't have to do with work at home. It is unprofessional to combine the two unless it is over a couple beers (after work).

Know when certain topics are appropriate. For instance, "someone who talks incessantly about her stay in the psych ward" would definitely be perceived as an undesirable trait in a financial adviser position, but it would be great for someone working in the mental health field.

This advice, like all of my other advice, is your choice. I am frequently wrong, and maybe in *your* situation it does make sense to chat about how awesome your mother-in-law is; go for it, but make a conscious decision that it is the right way to go, rather than just allowing it to happen.

Be productively busy

If you enjoy video games, I guess that is your thing. There are some positive aspects. Just know that, overall, it is making you dumber and is wasting your time. So is watching 99% of the TV programing that exists. Social media is a waste of time, as is spending more than a couple of hours a week "visiting" with any one particular "low-quality" person. Remember Jim Rohn's warning about becoming the average of the five people we spend the most time with? We become like them.

If you "chill" with a person that is not intelligent, thought-provoking, positive, educational, and motivational for too long, you are burning up your most irreplaceable resource; time. If you are sitting around drinking booze, smoking the marijuanas, and talking about sports, gaming, or repeating how much you both agree that something sucks, stop it. Actually, on a small scale, like an hour a week, go ahead; just don't waste too much time with that person.

> "I like being busy and juggling a lot of things at the same time. I get bored easily, so I need to do a lot."
> -Ellen DeGeneres

It is smart to categorize your minutes. Try it for a day or two, or better yet, for a week. What are you spending your time on? Did your time from 9:00 am to 9:15 am yesterday go into the "productive" category or the "wasted" category? Last night I sat on my couch with my wife for 3 hours watching "dumb" TV while consuming alcohol. I could

65

argue that we were "bonding;" however, the quality of bonding was very low compared to many other activities we could have been doing. We could have been doing productive things while bonding like writing a business plan, reading a book to each other, debating philosophy, bumping uglies, learning a new language, making a list of the things we are grateful for, or myriad other activities that add lasting value to our lives. TV and alcohol did not add any value.

The amount of time you choose to spend wasting time versus being productively busy is your choice. If I compare *what you know and what you have* now to *what you know and what you have* six months from now, I will be able to make a pretty good guesstimate of how much time you devoted to each category.

Think "Give" rather than "Take"

Doesn't this sound like the opposite of what I said about your duty being to get as much value as you can from the person that you are exchanging value with? Kind of, except that if you are still reading, you are smarter than 80% of people who buy this book. You are ready for *nuance*.

I once recruited a young man for our shooting experience business. I had observed him performing in his other job some months prior and thought that while he was not a polished superstar coach, he might be a good solid shooting instructor that would be reliable, grateful for the opportunity, and a hard worker.

As a college student, he worked in Jackson only during the summer, and as he left town for college, he stopped by for an initial interview and job description. The hourly pay I offered was to be three times more than he had earned at any job before.

I explained that I needed to "see him in action" working with guests and suggested that he come back to Jackson at his convenience to work a couple of shooting experiences with me.

He agreed, and in less than a month he suggested a period of three days he would be off from school and could make the 6-hour drive to Jackson Hole. We looked forward to meeting in a bit over a month.

Knowing that he was a "poor college student" I offered that he stay in our guest room and eat our food. I invited him to participate in a USPSA pistol match, using our gun, gear, and ammo for free.

I planned to give him some money to cover gas but did not mention it to him. I wanted to see how "invested" he was in this opportunity. I have in the last 25 years traveled for job interviews, and of course I always paid for my own hotel, flights, rental cars, gas, meals etc. I felt that I was being very generous.

I had cleaned the house, washed the sheets in the guest room, and made things nice for his arrival. Because it was a slow time of year, I scheduled "comped" experiences, just so that I could see him work with people. I knew this would cost our business a few hundred bucks, but I thought he just might be worth it.

The night before he was to arrive, he sent an email asking, "Will there be any kind of compensation to cover my costs this weekend?" My blood boiled and I almost hit reply to tell him the opportunity was off and not to bother coming.

If you are reading this and sharing my frustration, you likely have an entrepreneurial mindset and accept personal responsibility. If you think there was nothing wrong with his last-minute "entitled" request, you are probably stuck in the "E" (employee) mindset.

This isn't bad, it is just "different." Entrepreneurs need employees to carry out the job duties; you are a necessary part of the economy. I am, however, biased to like folks that see the big picture.

So, what would I have preferred to hear from this guy? I wanted him to appreciate that I was spending more to lure him onto our team than I have ever spent on any coach before. I wanted him to appreciate the opportunity and to show that he wanted to have some skin in the game as well. I wanted something that indicated that he was interested in the business, the opportunity, doing well, and getting the position.

Perhaps a few weeks before coming to Jackson, he could have sent an email saying, "Is there anything you suggest I spend an hour or two brushing up on to be well prepared for the groups we will be working with?"

Perhaps he could have sent an email saying, "Do you guys need anything from my town?" Perhaps an email saying, "I am really excited; anything else I need to know? What is the dress code?"

As it turned out, I liked, mentored, and have remained friends with him. He was simply unpolished, and he turned out to be a hard worker and not a "taker." Because of his initial attitude of "taking" rather than giving, he almost lost the opportunity to work for me, and for us to each benefit from each other's friendship.

The lesson one can learn from my example is that employers want their staff to be happy, supportive, and enthusiastic. Many employees are greedy and "in it" for themselves—and it shows. This is also true of many employers, and I suggest that the best working relationships are when all parties share a mutual goal and recognize and trust that their individual responsibility is to create value.

In my case, our current business's goal is to provide the best luxury shooting experiences in the world. We achieve this lofty goal by teaming with professionals who share our goal.

- [ ] Our best coaches show an "above and beyond' attitude. When they see a product that is related to shooting instruction and could make our business better, they email a link.
- [ ] When they see a cold weld chain link at a store that would work well for our steel targets, they buy a half dozen for us.
- [ ] When they see a piece of equipment that needs to be cleaned or repaired, they do so.
- [ ] They jump to our aid at a moment's notice. They do not complain about various types of clients.
- [ ] They make social media posts promoting our business on their personal accounts.
- [ ] They have positive attitudes and are fun to work with!
- [ ] They are genuinely "in our corner."

Have a good attitude

Attitude does make a big difference. Most of our staff in our shooting business have very high knowledge and skill levels and are excellent teachers, and a few also have an ego attached to their expert status. Most appreciate that our instruction is offered to all civilians, regardless of age, ethnic or national origin, etc.

Some coaches prefer shotgun shooting over pistols or rifles; however, we always appreciate SO much when the coach does not complain about the type of instruction requested.

The attitude of, "My next group is made up of first-time shooters from a big city who have teenagers, this is going to suck" is not healthy for that coach, nor is it good for the other coaches who feel his negative energy, either verbally or otherwise. We do not have coaches like that. (At least not *for long*)

The above example is for one of MY businesses. What vocation are YOU interested in? Think of the attitude regarding producing value that you should bring to work. Of course you want to invent the widget and you don't want to clean the toilet. Have patience, and cheerfully clean the toilet with pride.

71

Find a mentor

Most successful people want to help teach others. As you seek a mentor, stay a couple of steps above your level. In other words, ask a local landscape company owner for help, not the president of Ford Motor Company.

Don't make repeated bad decisions like complaining that you are "broke" and then eating out at McDonald's. Don't keep wasting your mentor's time. Your mentor will immediately know that you are full of it. A can of tuna and an apple are quite sufficient for a meal and can be had for less than $2.

So, what if you were born without all of the "advantages" I was? (I was reared in a single-parent home, often without running water or electricity. My mother took government welfare and I was never hungry, but we were VERY poor. At age 18, I had only completed 8th grade, and growing up, I did not have a father-figure role model to teach me about worth ethic, business and how to be successful.)

What if you don't speak well, don't know how to shave, are busy just surviving, etc.? **Contact me**. If I determine you are "serious" and are ready to get things done, I will help you get some mentoring. (shepardhumphries.com/harsh-resources)

I absolutely believe that some people are born into such crappy homes that they never realize that they can be successful and self-sufficient. I recognize that the inner-city sucks. I am sorry that your government has created that environment for you. There are caring people that seek to help you. Don't wait for them to search you out; make it happen on your own.

> *"It is your duty as a man to work. You must be industrious, or useless. It has been this way throughout history. If you are chipping rock, dividing papers, repairing machines, or directing engineers, you are fulfilling one of your basic duties. Also, you cannot support your family meagerly. 'You cannot wish for success; you must only earn it.'"*   -Nicholas De Laat, Esq.

Under-promise & over-deliver

I am always careful not to make promises I can't keep. I really do enjoy mentoring high-quality people, however I don't have time to help everyone in the world. I provide some private video training from time to time, and I will probably have a subscription-style offering sometime if I hear enough interest.

Tell you what, if you can figure out how to get a message to me, have the subject be, "I want mentoring" and you will be the first to know when I make time to do this project. I want you to create an incredible life, and I look forward to being your guide.

Section III

Don't Fall for Crap

You happen to live during a time of human history in which there is a lot of information available to most folks; however, 99% of people keep falling for a bunch of crap. Governments, churches, advertisers, parents, and various groups that have special interests, feed us stuff that is frequently junk.

The purpose of this book is to take the average young man who doesn't have the best prospects in life, and help him become great. Part of becoming great is seeing the world through a clear lens. This section is not directly related to you making an extra $2.50 an hour next year, but it *is* about you learning, getting smarter and seeing the world clearly. This *will* indirectly help you achieve your goals for the future.

Most folks who fill our world with bad information are useful idiots, and sometimes they mean harm. Either way, much of what you have been taught, both overtly and otherwise, is not true. I want you to examine everything that you thought you knew, judge it and throw out the junk. Gaining the ability for this kind of self-examination will help with everything we talked about in the previous two sections.

Useful Idiot

A useful idiot is a term for a person that propagandizes for a cause without knowing that they are simply a pawn. The term has often been attributed to Vladimir Lenin, but who knows.

Example: During a sermon titled, "Give God All the Praise" a preacher asks a wealthy member of his church if he believes that God has helped with his success. The wealthy guy says, "I give God all the praise." The preacher explains to the rest of his audience that they too can be wealthy if they tithe well and give God praise.

The wealthy guy was "used" to sell the idea of paying more money to the church. The preacher didn't care that the man deeply contemplated why he was wealthy, truth didn't matter. The wealthy guy was a pawn.

This section will alert you to a few methods and examples of things that, like Santa Claus, people either play along with or keep their mouths shut about. Like the Santa Claus lie, there are a bunch of people conspiring to fool you. Don't completely trust anything you hear, especially from me. Research and contemplate on your own.

We can not necessarily "do anything" about everything that surrounds us. We are "mid-stream" in our world. Governments exist. Collectivism exists. The **Most**

Dangerous Superstition exists. A lack of reason and logic exists. *I find it worthwhile to at least understand what is going on around me. It has helped me in life and business, and relates to all the stuff I taught you in the first half of the book.*

I might still allow the IRS to steal a quarter or third of the value vouchers that I have earned, but at least I don't submit mentally. There is a difference. Consider the woman who is beaten by her husband. She might be afraid to leave for physical reasons, but at least she knows he is an evil bastard. If he ever convinces her that she deserves to be abused, that is much more devastating.

If you are going to thrive in our crazy world, you must be able to identify "crazy." This knowledge isn't something we are born with, that is taught in school or that most families chat about over dinner. This stuff took me many decades to learn about.

I hope you find it beneficial that I dedicated half of this book to helping you learn about it more quickly than I did. I coil have saved many years of work that was not right for me had I been aware of these facts.

I want you to know when something is BS. Don't fall for common excuses. Don't fall for the common line of crap that the masses are fed. Be realistic and know what is happening around you. Knowing *how* to think will help keep you from being fooled into false "what to think" lies. Don't be a useful idiot.

Crisis

As part of their "non-binding" unofficial cozy partnership with Central Banks, which you will learn about in an upcoming section, governments create crises. The typical recipe is this:

A. Government warns of crisis A, with the help of the media.
B. Government offers a solution to the crisis.
C. Government requires that their subjects give up some freedoms "temporarily."
D. Government borrows money from central banks.
E. Government grows more powerful.
F. Government provides many sloppy "solutions" to the crisis and describes how bad things would have been if they had not intervened.
G. The crisis that was never that bad in the first place is forgotten.
H. The freedoms "temporarily" removed are not returned.
I. The central bank loans remain.

This scam is repeated with various crises, and each time, the less-informed 99% of civilization falls for it. While we must recall the wisdom of the stoics not to worry over that which we can not control, we do owe it to ourselves, as intelligent beings, to at least be able to spot the scam.

If you hone your observation skills, and improve your ability to predict what the bad guys will do, might this not put you a bit ahead? One example is the upcoming "need" to move to a centralized digital currency. Search the internet for James Corbett's perspective on this.

School

Do you want to be "schooled?" Are you another average fish that wants to go in the same direction as the rest of them? Are you a cog in a wheel turned by someone else. Knock it off!

Un-schooling yourself is tough. You probably attended a government school for 12+ years and maybe were foolish enough to go to college and waste four more of one of the most creative, energetic and opportunity-filled years of your life. Oh well, now it is too late, so it is time to move forward. Read "Skip College" by Connor Boyack and move on.

In school, you were taught to sit, stand and move from one room to another whenever a bell rang. You had to ask permission from another human being to relieve your bladder. This Prussian style of schooling is horrible. It helped make you believe in the myth of "authority."
Read The Most Dangerous Superstition by Larken Rose.

Larken's book also serves as a good IQ test. If you "get it" and understand the message, you have an above average IQ. If you read it and complain, "He didn't hand me an exact pre-packaged solution" then you are lower-IQ. This book is about the myth of authority, and it will help you see the world in a new and clearer way.

Schooling is not a particularly good way to get an education. I got a bachelor's degree while I was in my 20's—I think it was in Social Science—but it has been absolutely worthless to me. Really think about your options, and make an informed decision. In some cases, college is the best method to get an education, but most of the time it isn't. Don't let yourself fall for the lie that a lack of rubber-stamped, society-mandated schooling is what's holding you back from taking charge of your financial future.

> *"I've concluded that genius is as common as dirt. We suppress genius because we haven't yet figured out how to manage a population of educated men and women. The solution, I think, is simple and glorious. Let them manage themselves."* — *John Taylor Gatto, Weapons of Mass Instruction: A Schoolteacher's Journey Through The Dark World of Compulsory Schooling*

> *"School is a twelve-year jail sentence where bad habits are the only curriculum truly learned. I teach school and win awards doing it. I should know."*
> — *John Taylor Gatto*

Corruption in government schools

Beyond the more obvious problems of coercive state schooling are the little ways that corrupt governments team with companies to screw poor people. I will give two examples from my granddaughter's school in Tucson.

Recently, we picked my granddaughter up from her school and while there, took her to a "book fair" in a room in the school. As it turns out, a company called Scholastic Inc. ran this event and they run most "book fair" events at other schools too.

We told our 7-year-old granddaughter that we would buy two books for her. She selected a notebook for $12.99 that the Dollar Tree could have easily sold for $1 and made a profit. She selected another book on jungles that was $10.99. On the front of the notebook about Paris was a foam toy shaped like the Eiffel Tower. On the front of the jungle book was a patch of gold sequins meant to resemble a jaguar's fur. Is it any wonder that a seven year old little girl would be drawn to these?

This company is brilliant; they get to charge five times market prices and get the schools to do the work on their own property, making real estate costs zero for Scholastic Inc. I have not studied this company, I just saw a bunch of red flags.

81

The same school also frequently has school photo day. Not just once a year, but many times each year. Each time, children are ushered in front of the camera, cute photos are taken of them in kindergarten graduation gowns and the like, and each time poor families feel the pressure to plop down another $29.99 plus tax on another "best-value" 64-pack of photos. Once a year? I get it.

I am not opposed to books or photography. I want book publishers, authors, and photographers to make money. I AM offended, however, that just like payday loan places, they target poor people who are not financially sophisticated. I am including this warning in this book because I don't want you to fall for it.

Buy your kid's books at thrift stores, the Dollar Tree, Walmart, trade with another family in your neighborhood, or use free online exchanges. DO NOT feed the corrupt beasts like Scholastic Inc! For $26.07, we could have gotten ten MUCH better books anywhere but the school.

Yes, take a bunch of photos of your children, capture those moments. I suggest though that when you hire a professional, shop the market; it will not be your local school-photo-day folks.

"Follow the money." -Original source unknown

The jail industry

I am not finished talking about how corrupt businesses in a semi-socialist country like the US team up with governments to scam people. This time, the people to lose are the families of "captive audiences." The Prison Industrial Complex is a huge racket, and one that I used to financially benefit from.

The majority of the criminal justice system is a money-making scheme. One example of this is the scam run by the phone companies. A 15 minute phone call from someone in a county jail brings between $3 and $12 to the phone companies that have the best connections with crooked politicians. This is a better profit margin than casinos or governments!

There are a lot of companies that sell cots, spoons, tables, uniforms and other products and services that want the prison population to grow to 30% of the entire population. And just think about snacks and all of the other things that inmates and their families are coerced into buying.

This book is about getting *your* financial and productive life straight, so I will not wander too far from the core part that will help you. Long story short, don't go to jail. Don't have commitments with people that go to jail. You learned how to stay out of jail earlier in this book.

Some people get into the jail system at a young age and become comfortable in the organized chaos of the criminal justice system. Obviously, until a low-IQ lazy person has been well trained and institutionalized to enjoy being in jail, it is not pleasant.

Back when I worked in the Orange County jail system in Southern California, we deputies referred to visitors to the jail as "Inmates Out Of Custody." They were simply taking their turn being "on the outside," and we knew that pretty soon their cousin would be released, and they would be back inside. Currently, according to Wikipedia, almost three percent of adults in the US are in prison. Don't support their industry.

Theism

If you are a devout and faithful Christian, Jew or Muslim, this section is not of any use to you after this first paragraph. Really, peace be unto you; save your time and skip to the next topic, "Climate Change."

As described well at Why Won't God Heal Amputees, *your* religion only makes sense to people that are in it. You have your own jargon, "undeniable truths derived by faith," and way of thinking. That way of thinking is called faith. The opposite of blind faith is reason. Dear thesistic friends, and especially monotheistic friends, if your reason-based friends, coworkers and associates don't ask, don't tell! You will not know it, but what you say will sound absolutely ludicrous to them.

If being spiritual, religious or otherwise superstitious is serving you well and making your life richer, enjoy it! My goal is not to get you to pick reason over faith. Many faithful folks live rich and full lives, I am thrilled for my friends that do anything that makes them happy and doesn't hurt others.

If you have a high IQ, are not deeply involved in religion, and have an open mind, I suggest that you spend half a dozen hours on http://whywontgodhealamputees.com/. The world of religion that exists around you will make much more sense.

Climate change crisis

While we are talking about religion, let's look at the religion of sustainability. This is important because it is the wave of the future for the upcoming years, and understanding it will help you not only not fall for crap, it will also give you business and career ideas.

First of all, relax. The world is not headed for disaster. The Climate Change Crisis is a manufactured boogie-man created to scare us and control us. Obviously, climate changes by the second, minute, year, millenia, million and billion years. Nothing abnormal or scary is happening in nature because you prefer plastic straws. The earth's temps will rise, then they will fall. Wasting money on windmills is not helping the earth.

Because the UN is on board with the climate change crisis, all "progessive governments" and most big businesses are on board. Most people are useful idiots.

I think that the board of directors for the Holiday Inn chain honestly believes most of the crap they spew. They really think that sweet mother earth is about to implode, and that if they can lower the number of towels they have to wash, ~~they will be able to lower their operating costs~~ mother earth will be stronger. It is sad, and kinda funny in a mean way, to watch so many people with wide eyes tripping over each other to show who is the mostest greenest.

Your local spandex and helmet guy, the handsome one, full of energy, who is promoting a 5th lane, free government bike loan systems, and green bike lanes in your community? He really thinks he is doing good. He is very impressed with the charismatic speakers at the events he attends, and he honestly believes he is playing an important role in saving mother earth.

He does not realize that he is a useful idiot, doing exactly what those in real power want. Neither does the local bicycle mayor, college professor, cop, restaurant manager, school teacher or green-heating electrician.

Even though this troop of useful idiots is destroying human liberty and freedom and our way of life, don't hate them. They are idiots. Just like the German scientists that conducted research supporting Jews being animals were trying to do good by their god and country, so are these folks.

Beyond the intellectual satisfaction of not being a gullible sucker, why is this stuff important *to you*? Predicting future market demands can be handy for your pocketbook. I was silly enough to get into the small arms shooting experience industry, which has a very lousy future ahead.

Following is a partial list of what the bad guys who are in control want; these will be the trends for the foreseeable future:

1. There will be more "alternative" energy

2. Bicycles and other human powered transport devices will increase
3. "Public transportation" systems will grow
4. There will be fewer full-sized personally owned vehicles on the road
5. Populations will be coerced into living in cities close to public transportation
6. Our homes will be smaller and will have fewer conveniences
7. Our lives will be directed in a cookie-cutter fashion
8. "Plant based food" options will increase; cattle ranching will decrease
9. Communitarianism and collectivism will continue replacing individualism, likely through false flag events, taking advantage of crises etc
10. Government favors will keep the rich rich, and will make entrepreneurialism more difficult
11. Guns and other means of individual power will be decreased, humans will be tracked on their smart phones
12. Agenda 21 related tourism, like visiting ocean trash sites and volunteer work shutting down roads in "Wilderness areas" will increase

So, do some math. You know what the unseen hand that moves human critters around the chess board has planned. Would you be better off starting a bicycle repair business or a gunsmithing business? Should you invest in suburban properties or downtown property near the bus or subway station? As high-energy clothes dryers disappear, might a clothesline installation business be a good idea?

The advice of the stoics is to figure out what is in your control and what isn't. If you think you can stop the climate change crisis people's plans, go for it. Personally, I think they are too powerful compared to the amount of energy I am willing to expend combating them. I accept that they will do their thing and that it is out of my control.

Next, a stoic examination of what is right and what is wrong: parts of the sustainability crusader's plans are downright evil, like slipping birth control medicine into a third-world woman's compulsory vaccine injection. I do not suggest that you get a job holding women down while they are injected against their will.

Other things within the bad guy's master plan are not inherently evil, for example, the promotion of bicycling. Is it morally wrong to invent a more reflective type of paint to put on bicycles that helps motorists see them at night and avoid collisions? No, it is not immoral, and it could be very profitable, while also saving lives.

Yes, I am suggesting that you "join them" when it is not immoral. "They" want certain stuff, and creative minds that predict trends will do well. The Agenda 21 and 2030 folks are bad, stupid, manipulative and nasty; however, they are winning and you can jump on the wagon and make a bunch of money.

"Happiness and freedom begin with a clear understanding of one principle: Some things are within our control, and some things are not. It is only after you have faced up to this fundamental rule and learned to distinguish between what you can and can't control that inner tranquility and outer effectiveness become possible." – Epictetus

Collectivism, communitarianism and individualism

I mentioned a few words in this subtitle that are not commonly used. Let's take a quick look at them, and if the ideas interest you, I encourage you to investigate further while also recognizing that your priority is getting your life squared away in terms of food, housing, occupation, lifestyle, etc., first.

Collectivism is the concept that the needs and desires of the collective are more important than the needs and desires of the individual. If this sounds reasonable to you, I would venture to guess that you attended government schools and that you associate with fairly *normal* people. Our society has incredibly strong collectivist influences, including schools, your local paper, your church and many other organizations. What is wrong with collectivism and democracy?

A gang of rapists is a collectivist organization. If three of us want to rape the fourth person, democracy prevails with a 75% win for the rapists. If the woman complains, she is told that she is greedy and should share what she has with others.

> *"Democracy. Because the majority is always right." -Unknown origin*

Other examples of collectivist organizations are democratic governments and communitarian-based societies. With communitarianism, the concept is that the community "owns" the individuals in it, and the value they produce. Individuals are seen as "community assets," and the bad guys attempt to get all individuals to think this is a good thing.

Under communitarianism, these individuals are born into society with a perceived debt to others and must not seek out their own happiness, but rather must serve the community. Consider the idea of you being a plumber. Your plumbing work is a "community asset," and you are expected to provide your services, even if you don't want to. If you attempt to sell your services, rather than donate them as others want them, you are looked down upon.

The United Nations is enthusiastic about this concept. If you are interested in learning more, use your favorite search engine and the UN's website. Search for, "Plan of action to integrate volunteering into the 2030 Agenda for Sustainable Development Report of the Secretary-General."

Individualism is the concept that humans are born free, and that we may live the life we choose. When a government seeks to steal a portion of an individual's income that is to be used "for the community good," an individualist would argue that theft is wrong and that individuals may control their own lives and the products of their labor.

G. Edward Griffin and Rosa Koire have thought-provoking content on YouTube about collectivism, individualism and communitarianism. My philosophical journey began with minarchism and has progressed to voluntaryism.

Taxes / Theft

Taxation is theft. Governments have stolen from productive people for many thousands of years; it's nothing new. It will continue. How do you best prepare your life, knowing that many organizations exist that wish to eat you alive?

One smart idea that a friend of mine has adopted is "to have so much money it doesn't matter." Imagine how incredible life would be for you if you could have almost everything you wanted. Jet skis, a house, another couple houses, a handful of awesome cars, a fun little bush plane, vacations, etc. If you could have five or ten million dollars worth of this stuff paid off, and if you had an annual income of $250k, you could live a pretty awesome life, right?

At common investment return rates over the last many years, $8 million bucks would produce at least $250k per year in returns. When taxes go up though, more of that $250k will be taxed. Let's figure a 75% tax rate on capital gains. Better have $32 million making you money, right? So, $5 million in stuff and $32 million in investments will make your life pretty awesome regardless of what governments steal, right?

Another tactic is to "have nothing," or at least very little. Consider the Rockefeller family; a Google "net worth" search shows they have far less money than the Walton family, and yet they probably have much more money. Their trick is that they don't openly "own" stuff, rather, *they control it.* This is very helpful when we consider estate taxation. When a person dies, the government steals a large portion of their net worth before their family gets what is left.

The world thinks that $11 billion dollars is split between 170 Rockefeller family members. This small fraction of their real net worth is what they will pay estate taxes on. This ability to have most of their wealth sheltered is far more intelligent than being famously wealthy like the Waltons. Being famous puts a person in the spotlight. Hiding in the shadows is a wise way not to be seen by thieves. Volumes have been written on how to avoid estate taxes and other forms of theft.

As an example, the Rockefellers owned some property in Jackson Hole Wyoming over 100 years ago. They didn't need the land for farming, they simply love the unspoiled wide open spaces. They bought some cheap land, used some political influence and within a few decades over 200,000 acres were what is now Grand Teton National Park.

Guess how much property taxes would be on that land if it was privately owned by the Rockefeller family? They wanted a huge hunk of wild and beautiful land to look at through their cabin windows. They got it, and while they do have to share the park with tourists, they are getting exactly what they want out of the land, and it is not considered part of their net worth, nor do they have to manage the property.

If the land went up for auction in the free market, their family would more than double their net worth.

On a smaller scale, consider several of my friends who live a very humble lifestyle, at least outwardly. They have a crappy old house and a crappy old car, those poor, poor folks. Nothing to see or tax there, Mr. Mafia man!

I predict that by 2025, there will be a centralized digital currency system in the US. There will likely be laws saying that having cash is illegal, and that all assets must be disclosed and made controllable by the central authority. This will mean that the person who has $100,000 in gold coins in a jar buried in the back yard will no longer be able to sell them in the free market without being taxed.

There are many legal loopholes and illegal tricks that can help producers lose less money through government taxation. The thieves will come up with more tricks, and producers will come up with more ways to keep what they earn. I, of course, would never suggest that you do anything illegal. The Rockefellers didn't do anything illegal and neither have my friends who purposefully look poor. As you start building your nest egg, I suggest that you study ways to keep your hard-earned value vouchers.

> *"Property taxes' rank right up there with 'income taxes' in terms of immorality and destructiveness. Where 'income taxes' are simply slavery using different words, 'property taxes' are just a Mafia*

95

turf racket using different words. For the former, if you earn a living on the gang's turf, they extort you. For the latter, if you own property in their territory, they extort you. The fact that most people still imagine both to be legitimate and acceptable shows just how powerful authoritarian indoctrination is. Meanwhile, even a brief objective examination of the concepts should make anyone see the lunacy of it. 'Wait, so every time I produce anything or trade with anyone, I have to give a cut to the local crime lord??' 'Wait, so I have to keep paying every year, for the privilege of keeping the property I already finished paying for??' And not only do most people not make such obvious observations, but if they hear someone else pointing out such things, the well-trained Stockholm Syndrome slaves usually make arguments condoning their own victimization. Thus is the power of the mind control that comes from repeated exposure to BS political mythology and propaganda." — Larken Rose

Giving back to the community

Giving, as used in the term "giving back," is typically meant as giving a gift that is not obligated by contract, written or otherwise. This term has for many years disturbed me, and I will share my thoughts on this subject. My reason for examining what at first might appear to be only an issue of semantics is that I fear the acceptance of this term and the philosophy behind it is damaging to humanity's intellectual welfare.

I turned to a few online dictionaries and combined their knowledge to offer some definitions.

Give is defined as to "freely transfer the possession of (something) to (someone); hand over to" and "cause or allow (someone or something) to have (something, esp. something abstract); provide or supply with."

Back is defined in this context as "expressing a return to an earlier or normal condition."

Community is defined as "a group of people living in the same place or having a particular characteristic in common."

"Community" is an abstraction and should be recognized as appropriate in some contexts while not in others. Think "communitarianism." Let's look at some examples.

In August of 2005 four men sexually assaulted a couple of young ladies in Jackson, Wyoming. That same month, there were surely four people that donated to a different young lady's scholarship fund.

Two of these young ladies will blame "individuals" for their horrible actions, and one will credit her "community"

97

with her college funding success, not necessarily the specific "individuals" who actually donated.

Is it fair to say that the young women who were sexually assaulted were "raped by the community"? Of course not! Individuals do things to and for individuals, and the collectivist notion of "community" in this regard is very destructive.

This fallacy of removing personal responsibility is widespread and, in my opinion, very harmful. We don't blame individuals for criminally wasteful spending but rather the "City Council" or "Congress" or "County Commissioners." While these abstractions are often useful linguistically for expediency in referring to groups of individuals, they remove personal responsibility.

Each spring in Jackson Hole, there is a Community Cleanup in which a few hundred individual volunteers clean the debris from the roadways in our area. Comments and accolades about our "community coming together" are lavished.

In fact, our government jurisdiction of Teton County has a population of 21,000 individuals. Can we *really* congratulate the collective when only one out of every 70 individuals among them perform a deed? Of course not!

Understanding that there is a decisive difference between community and individuals that make up a community is very important. So that one does not have to say they live near John & Sue & Tina & Hank & Terri & 17,000 other names, it is certainly fine to say that one lives in the Jackson Hole community.

To say that the community cleans roadways, rapes, or gives to those in need is not intellectually truthful, however, and it is damaging because it removes personal responsibility, for the good and the bad. Individuals do all of these things, but again, "community" is simply an abstraction. Since a community can not give, it isn't possible to give anything back to a community.

To illustrate this concept, let's use Joe as an example.

> Joe was born in Mytowne to a poor family. He began shoveling dog poop at age twelve for extra money, and this led him to lawn mowing jobs as well. Some of his clients, A & B, recognized his work ethic and sponsored him on a high school ski trip. Another client, C, paid for him to attend a small business development seminar in Nearbytowne when he was 16. Meanwhile, 28 local hunters donated money to a shooting sports program that Joe participated in as a young adult. Some of these benefits that Joe received were based partially on merit, and some were simply because of a few individuals' goodwill.

At age 17, Joe got a job repairing windshields. He later quit to open up his own windshield repair business, which his retired neighbor, D, helped teach him to run. Joe began hiring employees and by age 25 had opened three branches of his windshield repair business. By age 30, he had built twelve other branches and had added oil changes and windshield replacements to his offerings. Joe now cleared over $400k each year. Joe donated $10k to the shooting program he had been a part of for the purchase of new guns, but took pause when a neighbor mentioned that he was "giving back to the community."

In fact, Joe was not "giving back" to anyone. He was simply appreciative of the personal growth and joy he had experienced through shooting and wanted other youth to enjoy similar feelings. He knew that each time he drove by the shooting range on a Tuesday evening and heard shots being fired, he would feel happiness knowing it was likely one of the guns he donated that was bringing someone else joy.

This new generation of youth included Tommy. Because Tommy had never "given" anything to Joe, it would be impossible for Joe to "give back" to Tommy. Joe considered that since Tommy was part of his community, maybe from a collectivist standpoint Joe WAS "giving back" but in fact this was not the case.

In our parable, Joe had received gifts from clients A, B, and C, neighbor D, and 28 hunters. If Joe gave a gift to any of those 32 people, he could be "giving back." Anything Joe gives to people other than those 32 is NOT "giving back" but instead is "giving."

So, why do I take such great offense to this "little linguistic error?" Participating in this deceptive language strengthens the untrue notion of community being separate from or greater than the sum of its parts. Because many have allowed this and other manipulations to be spoken without challenge, now the curious thinker who points out the error in thinking is labeled a curmudgeon. As people of new generations accepted these notions, they were more likely to expand the thinking to "community service" or "community organizer" or "community values."

The problem here is that we are again removing individuality and personal responsibility from the scenario. We should be teaching our children that the non-theist gay man down the street has his own set of values, as does the Baptist straight man the next door down, and that every person gets to choose their own values. Instead, with collectivism, we begin to extol the "community values" based on the most vocal and powerful 51% individual's preferences. These preferences are often the result of mindless absorption of "news" from an entertainment company like CNN, FOX or NPR. This demagoguery (leader of the mob agitating and directing the mob) is commonly accepted today and is manipulated by people on different sides of an issue.

Should we stop using the term "community?" No, we should simply understand that it is only an abstraction. It isn't a thing to help, be helped or be hurt by Joe or anyone else.

Should we stop "giving" to causes we like? No, we should simply understand that in almost all cases, we are not giving "back," and that we are not morally superior for giving. We especially don't get any moral credits for giving other people's money away. If you get joy by giving your time or money to other folks, that is fine. It does not make you better than someone else that uses their money in other ways.

So, when I hear my neighbors say, "That is great that the Waltons are giving back to the community," they can expect that I will engage them in vigorous conversation.

Silver Spoon Peers

Heck yes I am jealous of friends that have huge financial resources handed to them. I have a number of friends who financially benefit from their grandfathers' and father's financial successes. I very much wish that my parents had been wealthy.

I want "stuff" like retirement before age 80, a nice vehicle, a ranch to enjoy for business and pleasure, and much, much more. It would have been awesome if Mommy and Daddy had paid for my vehicle expenses, food, rent or tuition while in college. It would have been nice to have been gifted with the family hand-me-down car.

I have friends whose parents are deca-millionaires. Most don't fully appreciate how much they have financially benefited. During one stage of my life, I dreamt often of having a tiny portion of their cash drippings with which I could have started or grown my businesses.

In truth, though, the more I have seen my rich peers' lives unfold, the more I have concluded that getting "help" from Mommy and Daddy isn't necessarily good for a person in the long run. Knowing that a $65 broken part on your car will mean you don't have transportation for two weeks makes you drive more carefully and take better care of your belongings.

There is something about being very poor and barely scratching out a living that creates desperation and passion to take action so that life will suck less. I recall that before I was even ten years old, my mom encouraged me to walk ahead at the grocery store so that I would not have to witness her humiliation of using food stamps. That sucked.

> *"Hard times create strong men. Strong men create good times. Good times create weak men. And, weak men create hard times."* — G. Michael Hopf

I struggled for many years, and even when I had more money, it wasn't "big money." Yes, I can go out for a $150 dinner without feeling the impact; however, that is a very small threshold in relationship to the BIG luxuries I want. I figure that for my wife and I to be able to retire we need another $3.5 million.

So yes, I feel your pain. I wonder if anyone ever has "enough," because I guarantee that if I had $5 million handed to me, after the government stole their "fair share" and I had $3.5 million remaining, I wouldn't sigh with relief, throw my computer away and stop producing.

At this point in my life, I REALLY want land to use for a business project. I can afford to pay about five percent of what market rates would say I should. My concept is really a great idea for someone who has a mommy and daddy to subsidize it.

Instead of focusing on my jealousy and giving up, I have been grateful and excited beyond measure about each meeting I have. And by the way, getting meetings with kazillionaires isn't easy. I have immense gratitude for all of the opportunities I have had … and blown. I am proud to have created many of these opportunities, and luck also plays a part. I openly admit that I am still weak and wish one of the people I have asked for land use would "give me a break" and give me a "hand up."

But each time I ask another wealthy rancher, I hear another "no." Last year, a guy said that it would take a huge minimum payment for anyone to think about using his family ranch. This amount was small to him, and yet out of reach for me, making it a "no."

More recently, I received another "no" from the best land location, layout and logistical opportunity I have ever found. If you are reading this book, you are probably at a lower financial rung on the ladder than I am. You are likely reading my story and wishing you could even be a fraction of the way. Just like I'm wishing I were a few rungs higher myself!

You know what though? The rich sons and daughters of wealthy folks are not satisfied with their lives any more than we are.

Even if a person's parents have a $50 million net worth, they can't afford to buy each of their kids used high-end jets. A new Gulfstream G-650 is $65 million. This means that a person who has $50 million net worth—even if they were willing to spend half of it on a nice jet—can only look with jealousy at the G-650 buyer who pays cash.

If you are reading this book because someone that cares about you gave it to you, they want you to be successful. I wrote the dang book. Neither the person that gave you this book, you nor I have as much money as we want. I have opened my heart about my fantasies of the big day arriving.

That trust fund baby you know is not happy either. You and I would be well advised to stop being jealous. We ought to "buck up buttercup" and appreciate that we have some areas in our life that are ahead of our wealthy pals and some that are behind them.

My wife and I spent a bunch of money a few years ago to go to a week-long business mastery event with Tony Robbins. Yeah, you should be jealous. The 70% of the week that wasn't marketing upsells was awesome, and Tony said something that really made me think.

The story is of Cortez landing in Mexico with his soldiers, their goal being to conquer the land. Upon landing, Cortez ordered his soldiers to "Burn the Ships." This was a way of saying that failure was not an option. They did not have a "plan B." Their only option was to win. There are times to think like this, and there are times to have plan B's, just in case plan A doesn't work.

You and I can keep on being wimpy little dreamers, making $10,000, $100,000 or $1,000,000 a year, crying because we don't make that one additional digit. We can keep hoping that we will be able to help Bill Gates with his flat tire and as a way of thanks we will hand us a "thank you" gift of a billion bucks.

We can compare our "poor me" situations—perhaps not being able to buy our awesome wives a used G-650, or not even being able to buy her a $40 meal for our anniversary. In both situations, the disappointment is very real. Meanwhile, in countries whose governments have done what governments do for longer, and are further along that destructive path than the government that rules me, there are folks that are starving to death.

Recently a friend took me to dinner at my favorite restaurant in Jackson Hole, the Blue Lion. The $40-ish bottle of wine was excellent with my $14 appetizer and $48 entre. He enjoyed his similarly priced entre. How fortunate can I be? I am living *the good life*!

What have you experienced in the last week that was kinda nice? "Nothing man. I am broke," might be your response.

Guess what? You experienced more wealth and opulence in the last week than at least two billion other people. You didn't die, or watch a loved one die, from starvation, a lack of indoor climate control, or any of the other physical or social diseases that exist in collectivist societies. Be grateful!

Let's make a deal; I will man up and stop whining about not being able to find a three-mile long shooting area for a low price, and you stop whining about whatever YOUR current problem is.

Yes, Poindexter beside us got to go to college without working three jobs. Yes, Poindexter has a nice car. Yes, he has a nice place to live. Yes, his daddy's friend hired him to work in his company. I get it.

The truth is, neither you nor I will probably ever own a nice new luxury jet. We can, however, build a really nice life. If we quit whining, buckle down for a few more years and work 70+ hour weeks, live frugally, and create a bunch of value, we will be eating some really awesome racks of lamb at the Blue Lion. Now, let's get it done.

Banking

Debt. Don't do it. I know that the credit card companies are offering you what looks like free money, but it isn't free. It is very expensive. In almost every case, your life will be better if you never pay interest. Interest is good, but only when people pay it to you.

Getting a loan to buy a home is one exception, and a business loan is another exception. In the case of the house, know that the economy is great for about seven years (give or take five) then is bad for a while, then is good, etc. If you choose to buy a house, do so only when the economy is lousy.

Be careful about business loans. If a few banks have turned you down, it is probably a bad idea. If you tell a couple of wealthy friends about your incredible business and that you are considering getting a loan from the bank, and if they don't offer to loan you the money, your idea probably isn't a very "sure thing." Be careful.

Fractional reserve banking. OK, this is a very big deal. The banking system is purposefully made to seem complex; however, it doesn't have to be. The idea of a bank as a place where you put $100 into savings, and they loan that $100 to a business, is a sound idea. The business pays the bank 3% interest, the bank pays you 1% interest, and the bank keeps 2% interest. That is what most people believe happens. Nope.

Fractional reserve banking is the standard. In this system, the bank only actually has a fraction of the money that it lends, traditionally ten percent. You put $100 into savings, and the bank now loans out $1,000. They figure that you and the other nine people who each put $100 into savings will not want to withdraw your money at the same time; when that does happen though, it is called a "bank run."

Now, the bank is making their 1% interest on $10,000 and they only have $1,000 actual cash from you and the other nine people in their vault. Cool deal for them right? While fractional reserve banking is not an ethical or smart system, if all goes well and there is not a bank run, it can kind of work for a while.

Central banking. OK, you thought the fractional reserve scam was a neat trick? Check this out. A central bank forms a cartel of member banks. (Look up the word "cartel," and you will learn that it does not mean, "Columbia" or "drugs.") There are many central banks and parent organizations around the world, and they are mostly owned by just a few families.

Central banks have governments as their primary borrowers. One example is the current central bank in the US, which is a private bank called the Federal Reserve. This bank is the tail that wags the dog. Central bank owners are not really known, and any researcher who postulates the identity of the owner is labeled a "conspiracy theorist" so I won't even try. Also, I don't know who they are.

Let's chat for a moment about conspiracies. They exist. Remember the Santa Claus lie? Also, there are a bunch of wackos who think that everything is a conspiracy. If you and I conspire to rob a bank, and we are smart about it, we will not leave any real evidence. We will have alibis. If anyone accuses us of conspiring, we ought to call them a wacko and demand evidence. If we have half a brain, they won't have any evidence. If we have friends in the press, we could encourage them to label the wackos as wackos and accuse them of spewing fake news. If we are good at what we do, we will not ever be 100% busted, even though a few people will suspect the truth. But we did, in fact conspire.

Back to central banking; this is roughly how central banks work:
- Create a need that governments can use to scare their subjects with.
- Create fake "money" that exists on the little pieces of paper but is not backed by any real value.
- Loan the fake money to the government at high interest rates.
- Have loan restructuring systems in place so that the loan will never be paid off.
- Distract useful idiots from listening to whistleblowers.

This is an example of what central banking would look like in the real world:

> A family who owns the central bank in Bigtown and also the central bank in Smalltown will stir up trouble between Bigtown folks and Smalltown folks.
>
> After all, they will say, Smalltown is filled with bad people who want to hurt the people of Bigtown. Bigtown must show that they are the dominant power, because if they do so, Smalltown will not attack and there will be peace. Bigtown people care about their children, their god, their country, and peace. They want good for everyone and don't understand why the Smalltown folks are heathens that hate them so much.
>
> Meanwhile, the good people of Smalltown wonder why Bigtown folks are suddenly so mean and aggressive. After all, Smalltown folks enjoy time with their family, work hard, love their god and their country, and want peace. They wonder why Bigtown folks always want to stir up trouble.
>
> It is time for some good news, and the good news for the Smalltown folks is that their loving and generous politicians are willing to borrow money from their central bank to strengthen their military

so that they can defend themselves from the Bigtown military's imminent attack. Even frugal people in Smalltown recognize that at a time like this, they must come together as patriots to defend their loved ones and homeland. They support borrowing more money from their central bank to address this crisis.

Bigtown learns that Smalltown is buying more bullets and tanks, and wishes that Smalltown folks were not such radicalized insurgents, hell-bent on violence. Bigtown folks realize that at a time like this, they must come together as patriots to defend their loved ones and homeland. They support borrowing more money from their central bank.

The owner of the central banks hits the "print" key on both of his printing presses and spends about 23 cents on ink and paper costs to print out a $1 billion dolar bill in Smalltown currency and another $1 billion bill in Bigtown currency. The bank loans the money for only 10% interest to the governments of Bigtown and Smalltown.

The governments of Bigtown and Smalltown stir up the patriotism of their subjects and ask for the lives of their sons to go over to the other town to defeat the evil attackers, using the newly purchased tanks and bullets. How are the soldiers to be paid? Great news, the central bank has a heart and realizes that at a time like this, their town needs them during this time of crisis. They step up to the plate and do their part, loaning another billion bucks to their town's government for soldier's salaries.

Beyond the obvious problems with the above scenario, there is the fact that the printing of more of a thing causes each unit of that thing to have a lower value. This is called inflation. Inflation is when...

Wait, what? This just in! Smalltown is being inundated with peanuts from Averagetown. It is time for a war against nuts! It is a crisis!

How shall we fight this war against nuts? We need more government nut enforcement agents. These brave men and women lay their lives on the line to keep us safe from nuts, but they are understaffed and have lousy equipment. Isn't it time that the Smalltown government wrote some grants to help neighborhood government nut enforcement agents keep their neighborhoods safe? Our children are worth it, aren't they? To fund the grant, we must borrow more money from the central bank. Do you think they would be so kind as to hook us up?

This just in, our literacy rate is declining! We must fund education, but how?

What? The globe is warming? Should we not put aside our differences with neighboring towns and all of us borrow money from our central banks to fight this climate change?

Oh my! The people from the neighboring town are trying to sneak into our town. We must build a wall! How shall we fund it?

Oh no! COVID-19 will kill 2% of the world's population. Everyone stop working and producing and borrow money from the central banks!

Central Banks are one of the three biggest problems in the world today. You don't have to understand it all right now; just know that it is an issue. When you have time, after you have a comfortable income, start your inquiry by reading The Creature From Jekyll Island. In the meantime, there isn't anything you can do about it, so focus on making your life financially better.

Preparation, being a prepper

Will society and the government take care of you? No. They will not. They don't care about you. They are not your friends. They don't owe you anything. YOU are always one of the top few humans that cares most about you. YOU are responsible for preparing your life for bad times.

Sometime in the next 20 years, perhaps in a week, perhaps in 19 years, people in your geographic area will face a "crisis" (though I hope that in 2040, I will have been proven wrong). This could be a high unemployment rate, an oppressive gang, whether criminal cartel or government, or it could be a natural disaster. You will likely "lose" your primary sources of income, your housing situation, your wealth, and your privacy, liberty and freedom.

Worse yet, it could be caused by a group of bad people wishing to control you, extract value from you by force, or kill you. The most efficient way for these folks to do so is not as an openly obvious criminal gang like the Mexican cartel, but rather by claiming to have authority over you. The United Nations, Council on Foreign Relations, the World Bank, the World Health Organization, all governments, most religions, and other similar groups will attack.

Frequently, their attack is a psychologically smart attack. They will create a crisis and offer a solution, and the solution will always reduce your freedom, privacy and wealth. *Have you ever seen something like this happen in our society?*

Tough times throughout history have occurred when governments have fooled their subjects into going to war against other fooled subjects who were egged on by their masters. Other times, people/organizations like Genghis Khan, the government of England, the government of the US, and many others have sought to take over the lands and people in various geographic areas.

Read history. Learn about central banks and the nature of government to learn how these tough times come about. (See the reading list Appendix 1 in this book and search online for my updated suggested reading list.)

Regardless of what the "problem" is, you will face personal and societal crises in your lifetime beyond whatever crisis drove you to this book in the first place. This book is not meant to be a complete guide to prepping, so I will offer only a few ideas to get you started.

To survive, humans need water, talent, warmth, defense, a good mindset and food. This book is primarily about the "talent" piece, the part having to do with your skills, knowledge, ability, production and character.

Water is very important. Your plan A is the faucet in your house, plan B are local stores. What are your plans C through F? Do you have lighters, wood and pots for boiling water? Do you have a nearby source of water? When it dries up, what is the next source? Do you have a Big Berkey water filter, buckets, jugs, iodine tablets and other plans?

Warmth is not a concern for my friends in Acapulco. If the climate where you live gets cold, how will you stay warm? Clothing and blankets are a good solution, and so is having multiple ways to heat your living space when the electricity or public gas lines don't provide their service. Wood fires and gas stoves have been most popular throughout history.

Defense is a basic human skill every person should have. The job often goes to males; are you prepared? Do you have basic martial arts skills, backup locks for your home, a hiding place "safe room" with the other people in your household, firearms, ammunition, training and a plan? You'd better (as your masters allow by their laws). Do you have a plan with trustworthy, loyal and capable people to survive 24/7 dangers from multiple directions?

Are you mentally prepared for tough times? Can you stay cheerful and keep a positive attitude? Can you keep being a good, productive and principled human being when the SHTF? Learn about stoicism; spending an hour a week for a few months will help you learn some great skills. My mental state would not be as elevated as it currently is if I didn't watch a couple videos each week by the Daily Stoic.

We can live without food for weeks, however it is a very handy fuel for our bodies and is also good for our emotions. A full belly at least 3 times a week is a great way to live. A full belly 24/7 is not good. Consider how you will get food if things go poorly. Every human should have a six-month or greater supply of food in their home.

Spaghetti, pasta, rice, dried beans and canned meat will allow you to survive. Two people can "survive" on half a pack of pasta and a shared can of tuna each day. One person can live even better on the same amount. How many days worth of food do you have in your home right now if you rationed yourself to one small meal a day? What about two better meals each day? Your neighbor will probably have less than a week or two of food, especially if they don't have the mindset and plan to ration themselves. Your stash is their best bet for food, so if you don't plan to share your stash with everyone - don't tell anyone you have it. Don't tell them you have toilet paper, either! Think about defense again.

This was a very short run-down of prepping, and I encourage you to take this issue seriously now - not after you have that 1000 otz. that we talked about earlier. This issue can and should be worked on concurrently with your efforts to build your financial future." Don't wait until next week when there's a run on toilet paper and beans. Search the internet for information and opinions or ask a Mormon friend for a guide to prepping. See Appendix 3 for a recent article I wrote with more specific prepping advice.

Most people are ignorant

I don't say this to be mean; I say it as a warning to save you time and effort. If you have read this far, you have clearly gleaned some value from it. You will likely suggest it to a handful of friends, and out of every ten people you suggest it to, nine will not read it. Then all nine will whine in a year about how they are "broke."

As you study history, human nature, government and other topics, you will try to share what you learn with others. Most will reject the knowledge, remaining willfully ignorant. Bottom line? Move on. You can not save everyone. Know that many people who you once held close will sometimes even become an enemy of truth and reason.

Propaganda

Propaganda exists. Look up the definition. It isn't a wacko conspiracy theory; it has been used the world over for many thousands of years. I have "fallen for" various forms of propaganda many times and will likely still fall for things again.

Propaganda is rarely easily noticed;it takes a keen eye to find it. An example is the slogan, "Don't Mess With Texas." This was a propaganda slogan that was part of a campaign created to stop littering in Texas. Check it out. One year ago, I didn't have any idea that the slogan was not an "accident," and I didn't even know that it referred to littering. Nonetheless, it has been in my brain for years as one of the things that I think about when I think of Texas.

In the above example, I am not suggesting that I am opposed to the message delivered through that propaganda. I hope that you never litter in Texas or anywhere. My point is that we should hone our senses and be on the lookout for propaganda.

Many of the information sources available to you offer propaganda. Many of the people spreading it are "useful idiots." The sign of a brilliant and well-funded propaganda campaign is when it can take on a life of its own.

For example, I am writing this section of your book in late March 2020, and governments very much want people to stay home due to a virus that is spreading. I am guessing that a hip DJ on a Top 40 station right now is encouraging people to stay home. The DJ does not have any more information than his listeners. He has bought into the propaganda.

In March 2020, several relatives sent me a "home video" of a Detroit nurse talking about the latest virus crisis. She violated many logical fallacies, displayed eye movements congruent with dishonesty, included click-bait terminology, and pleaded for people to obey the government's rules. I suspect that her performance was scripted; however, my point is true even if it wasn't. 98% of people who are not experts in the subject of propaganda will see her video and will think it was spontaneous, true, righteous and good.

Thousands of other people are also following the master script—just like the DJ and the nurse in the video—most without even knowing it.

In a few months or years, a new "thing to fear" will come to consciousness, perhaps the dangers of Canadians, health food, or book-reading. Maybe even all three? The government will declare an emergency and offer a solution to the crisis. The solution will include permanent removal of "rights" and more loans from central banks.

The government will warn us to "watch out for Canadian health food books" and a bit later, due to the emergency situation, will make new legislation. Because all subjects failed to voluntarily comply and hate Canadians, books, and health food, the government will "have" to protect us by taking more drastic steps. The DJ will speak with passion about the dangers, and we will know that all of the cool people are not ignoring this grave danger and are instead actively supporting The Response.

The Jews or Japs, the marijuanas, the Muslims, the climate, the purveyors of fake news, the AIDS, the second-hand smoke, the COVID-19 or some other really scary threat will always be just over the hill, heading our direction, and "our glorious and benevolent government" will take action.

They will spread the news through contemporary channels and methods, and most people will fall for it. You won't.

Why does this matter and what can you do about it? I don't know. The groups of people calling themselves governments are powerful, they all suck, and you are probably doomed. What can one person do? I don't know, but they tell me knowledge is power.

Good talk.

Seeking and Sifting for Truth:
Navigating through a world of misinformation

> *I am including this recent article I wrote for THE*
> *VOLUNTARYIST, even though I have already*
> *introduced some of these concepts throughout this*
> *book. I hope that reexamining some points, this time*
> *with the mindset of finding truth in our world, will*
> *be of value to you.*

Earlier this month, I visited a voluntaryist pal in Nevada. He is an older fellow and has led an interesting life, including mining the claim he inherited from his grandfather near Cherry Creek. We chatted about dowsing, alternative medicine, sifting rocks through a mesh to only let the correct ore pass through, conspiracy theories and many other topics. Flynn and I both yearn for the truth and do not wish to be hoodwinked by false versions. Throughout our lives, we have observed some people providing dishonest information in a very convincing way.

I decided that it was time to contemplate more deeply how I arrive at my conclusions, principles, values and worldviews. Join me as I examine how we think (reason), how we argue (logic), and how we examine data (scientific method).

Reason and logic

Reason and logic are important to me. I attempt to live a stoic life, and I have discovered that combining reason, logic, and the scientific method provides a pretty accurate way to observe the world and draw conclusions. I also appreciate the subconscious, and I know that my front brain's analytical nature can also benefit from the much more powerful back brain.

Having mentioned the tools that I use in discovering the world, let's enjoy a crash course on reason, logic, and the scientific method. Many people that teach the use of these tools are not "people-people," and their personality types lean more toward the engineer/scientist/analytic type of person. I am better at drinking beer at barbecues than understanding how to write a proper bibliography. My hope is that my lay-person approach and communication style will appeal to you regardless what type of person you are.

Familiarity with errors in reasoning is very important. Reason and logic have more to do with the structure than the content. Something can be logical and reasonable, and at the same time "false." Say, for example, a fictional character named Bill declares that, "I like joy and I think joy is good." If Bill gets joy from kicking puppies, then logic and reason would allow him to say that according to his worldview, kicking puppies is a valid behavior. According to the structure of reason and logic, Bill's argument is sound, even though abhorrent to most people.

If we want to argue with Bill, we must first decide which of his premises we share. We must not attack, either in our thinking or in our critique, the solid parts of Bill's argument. As it turns out, we agree with Bill that we also like joy and that joy is good. But we do not share his premise that kicking puppies brings us joy. We simply have different values and worldviews than Bill about what brings us joy. These can be very strong beliefs based on our values, or can be casual preferences.

In this example, Bill has different values in terms of kindness to animals than we do. I do not like Bill's actions, and while his arguments might pass the tests of logic and reason, they can still be "bad" and "wrong" from my perspective. We can either persuade Bill to change his values, or, if he refuses, we may decide to take some other action.

Easy stuff, right? Kind of. Most government schools do not teach the topics of logic or reason. A good starting place to understand errors in reasoning and conclusions is a review of logical fallacies, which are easily found online. It is important to be familiar with them, even if we don't recall their names. Let's continue with Bill's ridiculous example and imagine that we tell Bill that we value being kind to animals and not kicking them. Bill might retort, "So basically you think animals should be able to get away with anything, even biting a harmless child without provocation." What Bill just did was create a Straw Man argument. He built an argument that is ridiculous and easy to defeat, and pretended that it was part of our argument.

Knowing that the above fallacy is called a "Straw Man" is not important. However, knowing that his argument is faulty and is potentially fallacious is important. I suggest that you learn about a new logical fallacy every morning for a month. In this way, within 30 days, you will be better versed than 99% of most people. There are many other fallacies that you should understand, including the Bandwagon Fallacy (also known as democracy), Circular Reasoning, and Causation versus Correlation.

I have mentioned reasoning, logic, and the scientific method as valuable, but what are some of the means of acquiring knowledge that I dislike? First would be the absence of any system. Secondly, ideas commonly called "they make me feel good" are of little use to me. "In my 58 years of life and 35 years of marriage, no car or woman has ever felt more right than that Corvette and that 23-year-old waitress I met yesterday." Feelings are important in interpersonal relationships and examining one's own self. However, they are a poor way to make important decisions or to arrive at important conclusions.

Scientific method
The modern scientific community has a number of systems and tools to evaluate the things they examine. One of these tools is the "scientific method." The scientific method has a number of steps that must be followed to examine a

question, including forming a hypothesis, systematic observation, measurement, experiment, and the formulation, testing, and modification of hypotheses. In many modern legal systems, there are "rules of evidence" that also serve as an objective system of observation. As a businessman, I appreciate systems, and I also allow for some flexibility so long as the structural stability remains intact.

Frequently, we do not have time, interest or energy to do all of the research on a topic for ourselves. We decide instead to turn to trusted experts. Do we really want to individually test which rubber compound makes the best windshield wiper? Do we really want to research all things that we have slight curiosities about? Of course not.

This creates a challenge in that many experts shape their truths to suit those who pay them. A couple excellent examples are drapetomania and climate change. When overt slavery existed in the US, the federal government had fugitive slave laws which legalized the forced return of escaped slaves to their masters. A doctor who practiced in the deep South in the mid-1800s invented a medical condition labeled "drapetomania," which he conjectured was the "condition" that made slaves want to run away.

In the first part of the 21st century, world governments are pushing the concept of catastrophic climate change. A researcher with a hypothesis suggesting humanity does not need to worry about climate change, would not receive funding for her research projects. The scientific community knows that the only acceptable results of their "studies" must include the existence of man-caused climate change and that action must be taken now!

In these two examples, we see that we cannot fully trust everything that credentialed scientists and media-approved "experts" say. Who then do we trust? Do we trust conspiracy entertainers, governments, people with government board-approved doctorates, quacks, salesmen or preachers?

Conspiracy theories

"Hillary Clinton is really an alien, and most of the mass violence incidents are fake." I find these to be ridiculous statements. I do not believe that a large percentage of political rulers are pedophiles. I do, however, believe that people conspire for both good and bad purposes. Conspiracy, as it pertains to our discussion, can be defined loosely as, "some folks chatting and planning about doing something."

Most conspiracy theories violate the rules of logic, reason, and the scientific method. However, is there ever a reason to believe something that is not 100% provable? Yes. I believe so.

Imagine that you and I, and three of our trusted friends had speculated in the "right" crypto-currency, and now find ourselves to be among the five wealthiest people in the world. We would spend and invest our money and still we would each have many billions of "extra" money. Is it possible that we would meet up and chat for a few days about how we might pool our money to create a better world for others? Is it possible that we would not want to be bothered by beggars and main-stream media, and that we might want to meet in private and all agree to sign a non-disclosure agreement? Might we agree not to record or document anything we discuss unless necessary to carry it out? Whether we and others have good or bad intentions, people do sit down and chat.

Not everything that is true is provable to everyone. Not everything that happens leaves evidence. Books like THE CREATURE FROM JEKYLL ISLAND by G. Edward Griffin and THE UNDERGROUND HISTORY OF THE AMERICAN EDUCATION SYSTEM by John Taylor Gatto are two examples of books that do not pass the scientific evidence test, but that are well worth reading. On the other hand, governments and others put out a massive amount of information that is designed to make a listener believe their falsehoods. Much disinformation is spread using modern persuasion and propaganda strategies. This is sometimes done maliciously, sometimes as a prank, and sometimes accidentally.

Snake oil salesmen sell medical cures, preachers sell salvation, bankers and governments sell fear and war, and many use similar techniques. I suggest you study propaganda, persuasion, sales, and the structure of multi-level marketing. The more you learn, the more easily you will be able to spot someone using strategies that just might not be trustworthy.

In my study of propaganda and my observation of mass communication tactics, I have been impressed with the proclamations of governments and mainstream media that their truths are not to be questioned. Of all of the professions, one of the least trusted is that of politician, and a close second is "government employee." It is a brilliant persuasion strategy to claim to be the only reliable source of "true" information.

From governments that accept drapetomania, to those that encourage the fear of climate change, to the ones that require politician worship, how are we to sift through all of the junk to find the nuggets of truth? My friend Flynn has spent countless hours crushing ore to sort out the tiny amount of gold that exists within. It was not easy for him and it is not easy for us.

How do voluntaryists think in the free market of information?

I have observed that most people that arrive at the philosophic destination called "voluntaryism" get there through sound thinking. Voluntaryism, which I define as a worldview that includes belief in, and a preference for, non-violent or non-coercive social situations, does not require others to think well. However, it seems that most voluntaryists do so.

I have also observed some people that identify as voluntaryists that do not think well, or have areas in which they depart from their good thinking processes. In most cases, as I speak with someone that believes in lizard people, that the earth is flat or other unproven things, I learn that they are not in fact defining voluntaryism as I am. I find that they think voluntaryism is simply, "I think differently than most folks, you think differently than most folks in other areas, so if you are a voluntaryist, I think I am as well." This faulty reasoning exposes that the person is not in fact a voluntaryist, at least by my, or common definition.

The free market allows for lousy thinking methods. The popularity of mega-lotteries, which some joke are "a tax on those that don't understand statistics" is an example of faulty thinking being a "winner" in the marketplace. There is room in the entertainment marketplace for wacko conspiracy theorists who charismatically "expose the truth" about their favorite topics. The free market is a concept, a process, and an open system. There is no management staff at the head of the free market offices promising a perfect outcome. What the free market and voluntaryism do reject is the idea that violence or its threat can win an argument. It has been said that "you can't shoot a truth," and "if he who employs coercion against me could mold me to his purposes by argument, no doubt he would. He pretends to punish me because his argument is strong; but he really punishes me because [his argument] is weak."

This brings us full circle to recognize that we are each responsible for our own beliefs and how we arrive at them. When the screaming YouTube host says that the Corona Virus is making unicorns come to life, and that the government is hiding the truth, it is up to the receiver of this "information" to decide how to evaluate it. Do you need a mid-sized city zoologist to say it is true? Do you need to see a photo of a unicorn, handle unicorn poop, or is there some other proof that you require? Again, there will not be hard evidence for every single thing that has ever happened, and you get to choose the facts that appear correct to you. If you decide that the man with the hoarse and urgent voice on YouTube is correct, no one will prevent you from building a unicorn defense fence around your home. There is no president of the free market that will warn you not to spend your money that way. While these silly examples seem harsh, and it is clear that the smart people will do better than the dumb people. This is how the real world works. You pay your money and you make your choice!

You may buy unicorn fencing, you may buy the quack's sagebrush vinegar potion for which he gives you anecdotal evidence, and you may buy lottery tickets. Tools exist to help us think better. Reason, logic, the scientific method, and an understanding of statistics, history, and economics can hone your thinking abilities. It is likely, for psychological reasons, that you will "feel better" taking the potion (or a sugar pill), and that the person with a unicorn fence will indeed live many years free of unicorn attacks. So long as we each accept responsibility for our choices, and so long as we do not coerce others to take actions based on our own personal preferences, we may enjoy an exciting voluntaryist life and live with happiness, relishing the many nuggets of golden knowledge we find.

My undergraduate degree is in social science, and my 20 years of casual study since has helped me to better "mine" for truth. I am sorry to disappoint you, but I do not have a fail-safe solution for sorting out the "gold nuggets" from the "fool's gold." The best any of us can do is use our common sense to apply logic, reason, and the scientific method, and then introduce an occasional dose of gut-check and intuition into our search for the truth.

When I read an article, I hope that the author can tie a neat ribbon around all the questions and answers that have been discussed. My ribbon is humility, and I will now tie it into a nice bow around this article. We have eyes, ears, noses, tongues, and skin, all of which send information to our brains. Then we make meaning out of it, and nearly always, the meaning we make out of it is not 100% accurate. Our past can interfere. Our preferences can interfere. A lot of other things can interfere, so how can we know what is true? It's okay with me that I can't know. I have working assumptions and whenever I need to, I update them. If I update one, it means I'm accepting that my previous views, which I've held for almost 50 years now, were wrong. I was wrong. And that's okay, because I can update my working assumptions.

Section IV

Starting a business

Starting a business is something that I think every human should do at least a couple of times, even if you decide that you are better suited for the "E" quadrant. You will learn so much by starting a business, even if it fails! Let's begin with an example.

Find a market need, often called a "pain point." For example, people do not like picking up dog poop from their yards, so you might decide to solve this pain point; you decide to start a pooper scooper business.

What are some important questions you should answer as you consider this business? As you read the questions below, and my thoughts, be thinking about a business that *you* could start, and make up some answers for that unique business.

Investigation into the business

What services will I offer?
Pooper scooper service for dog poop in yards. Possible expansion into cats, birds and other pet cleanup services?

How long will it take to do each job and get to the next one?
If you pick up poop from a specific backyard every day, it will only take two minutes per day for the cleanup. If you do it twice per week, it will take three minutes, and if you do it once per week, it will take five minutes. The job will take half again as long for each dog above one that is being cleaned up after.

Who is my target market?
Not everyone can afford to pay for a service like this. The poorest 75% of my city would never consider it, and retired people probably love doing yard work like this to fill their time. You might think that only busy professional people making over $100k a year would use this service.

You are dirt poor and don't have a car, so you can not drive long distances between clients. You decide that the Woodbridge community would be your best option to start with. It is an easy 45 minute bus trip from your friend's house where you are crashing on the couch.

How much will my equipment cost?
You will need a box of single-use rubber gloves, plastic bags and a scooping device. This will all be less than $20.

How much will it cost to keep the bad guys away?
(Business license, protection fees, sales tax, other permits, environmental impact studies, licenses and fees)

Neither the author nor the publisher suggest doing anything illegal. Having proper permits in place is recommended. Thieves, both government and private, enthusiastically target producers of value as their victims. Remember the stoic advice not to worry about what you can not change.

It is likely that the city in which you live has a business license requirement. It will likely cost $60 to $250 for a tiny business like yours.

If you live in a country that has a competing cartel in place, like Mexico, these fees might be double. Both the city and the other cartel organizations are, in essence, demanding your money in exchange for not harming you. This harm can either be physical, like breaking your leg, or financial, like fining you.

We learn that in your city, a business license costing $150 is required prior to starting a business. You didn't actually identify yourself or the type of business that you plan to do. Rather, you had a friend call the government and ask about a private hedge trimming service. This allows you the flexibility to later decide if you will acquire a license or work in the shadows. If you had made the call to the government yourself, you could be in bigger trouble if you get busted providing value to people without a permit.

Many state-level governments require businesses to demand money from your clients that you then hand over to the state. This is called "sales tax." Some states have an exception for services, while few have exceptions for products. In this case, we learn that your state does not require us to steal from our clients. Yay!

You learn that you don't have to join any "boards" or trade unions, so our grand total startup cost to keep the bad guys away is $150. Some entrepreneurs wait to be sure their business will work before buying a business license, even though this is not legal.

Who is my competition?
You check around town and learn that nobody else is doing this specific service. You also learn that landscape companies *do* handle this when they mow; however, the standard mowing schedule in our town is every 10 days. You learn from your friend's cousin, who works as a landscaper, that he hates dealing with dog poop and wishes his clients would use your new pooper scooper business.

How much money is reasonable to charge?
Beauty is in the eye of the beholder. Pricing is similar; long story short, price is determined by the market, in other

words, what someone will pay for a service or product and what someone is willing to accept in exchange for the product. This is an unknown market, so who knows?

A nice car costs about $30k when purchased brand new. The rancher reading this says, "nope, my last pickup was $75k," and the fancy Los Angeles Realtor laughs and says that her nice new car was $300k. To a government bureaucrat that is paid big money, is very stressed out, and is lazy and wants to feel important, poop-scooping is worth more than it is to a rural home-schooling family with 3 capable teenage kids.

What is your fictional situation? Last week you made no money, the week before that you made no money, so even if you could make $100 each week, that would be a real step up. Hmmm, you might start at $5 per cleanup visit.

How should I market my service?
Marketing should be effective. Word of mouth is generally the best marketing for this type of business. Sometimes annoying marketing is also effective. An annoying marketing technique is the hanging of flyers on doors.

You could put something on Craig's list, build a free website, have business cards made, have custom pens made or 3000 other ideas. You will test several methods and document the results. You will also definitely need to do some "cold call" sales.

Am I good at cold call sales?

If you can master cold call sales, you will be wealthy. "Cold calling" refers to contacting someone who has not expressed interest/asked for information, introducing yourself and your service, and persuading them to buy. I am an expert at this, but for many years have had a subconscious aversion to doing it. I would have a much higher net worth if I got over my issues. Are you willing to do what it takes? If so, you will make at least five times more value vouchers.

Launch

No, really, just launch. No more planning for this business; Let's get it done.

> As we discussed above, You need $12.99 for the rubber gloves, $1.06 for some trash bags from the Dollar Tree, $1.06 for a little trash container from the Dollar Tree, and $1.06 for a pickup tool from the Dollar Tree. All told, an investment of less than $20.

> You have exactly zero money to start. You know that you can find a way to get $5 bucks, so you decide to accept the risk of disease and skip gloves for your first couple jobs.

After purchasing our equipment, you head home and watch YouTube videos, including Storybrand One Liner Exercise by Donald Miller, some Tony Robbins, some Shark Tank, The Profit and some Ryan Holiday. You are being "productive" for as many hours of the day as you can, even though you are not being paid for these hours.

After doing some stretches and pushups, you shave and put on the business attire you purchased from the thrift store. You are ready for work. The trash bags and scooper both fit into the trash can, so you take them and head over to Woodbridge in the evening, arriving at about five o'clock pm.

You walk along a street with a huge welcoming smile on your face, your shoulders thrown back. After all, you are a proud, self-employed small business owner with a very valuable service to provide.

You wave at the people arriving home from work, and when you see someone getting out of their car you call out a cheerful, "Beautiful day, huh?" When a person walking their dog approaches, you ask if you can pet their dog. As you pet, you compliment them on some great attribute of their dog and ask its name. You explain that "I love dogs, and actually, that is why I am in the neighborhood. Many people don't like cleaning up doggy poop, so I have a service picking it up a couple times a week for them so that they have clean lawns and can spend their time enjoying the less-poopy time with their dog."

You don't try to sell to them at the moment; it is likely that you will see them again every evening at this time walking Wally. You continue walking and see some dog poop on the ground, so you stop and pick it up. A bit further along you notice a trash can laying on its side, so you stand it upright again.

You notice which houses are occupied, which are not, who is home, who has kids, who has dogs, who eyes you with suspicion and who doesn't. You are basically a very nice and helpful person. One lady gets out of her hybrid and challenges you as to why you are in the neighborhood and before you can answer tells you that if you don't live there you should leave. You smile and wish her a good evening as you keep walking. (You sure are glad you shaved, combed your hair, and wore a shirt that covers the tattoos you plan to remove!)

You see a family getting out of the minivan with the kids wearing soccer outfits, and you smile and ask, "Good time at soccer today?" A bit further you see a man getting his garbage can from the street and you wish him a nice evening. He is friendly and asks if you are new to the neighborhood.

"Yes," you tell him, "I don't live here, I work here with my service. Many people don't like cleaning up doggy poop, so I have a service picking it up a couple times a week for them so that they have clean lawns and can spend their time enjoying the less-poopy time with their dog." You wish the man a nice evening and keep walking.

So, not a single sale. How depressing, right? Well, kind of, except that today, unlike yesterday, you provided value to the world. You brightened people's day, you stood the trash can up, you made Wally happy, and you met new people. What an awesome day!

The next evening, as you are walking in Woodbridge, you see the nice person walking their dog again and you call out with joy, "Wally!" You greet Wally like the old trusted friends that you are and chat up Wally's owner a bit more, learning about him.

You continue this behavior, learning your target market and creating value. You will need to start making sales soon, and this might not be comfortable for you.

I am good at "sales" and I have more knowledge than most people, but I have always been scared to ask for the sale. You may not be afraid and may close your sale more easily than I do, I should learn to be as brave as you are!

Now you have launched, congrats! I encourage you to continue writing the above story in your mind with yourself as the protagonist; what pitfalls will you face? What fresh ideas do you have? Which of the actions I imagined above were different than what you would have done?

The primary goal of a business is to make a bunch of money as a result of providing a bunch of value. The good news is that even if the business fails as a money-maker, you will reap huge benefits. You will know what works and what does not work. You will discover 20 things that you will now know that you should never do again! You will make many mistakes. You will find that some of my above advice wasn't worth a darn, some was wrong, and some was pure gold.

Starting a business is difficult, time-consuming, frustrating, and rewarding. Like other important things in life, it will provide you with huge ups and huge downs. Your second business will hone your skills even more, and your third business will be even better. Wash, rinse, repeat. A dozen or so businesses later, you will probably have a big winner!

Parting words

If you spend 30 days following 20% of the advice I offer, and if you are doing it well, and you still don't have a job, YOU are likely the problem. Even that small 20% will dramatically improve your life. Yes, following 80% of the advice will be even better, however, as you will learn from 80/20 Sales and Marketing by Perry Marshall, working on the 20% that will make 80% of the difference is very efficient.

As I write today, in April, 2020, we are a month into the latest "crisis." This time it is COVID-19, a flu-like virus. I menton "this time" because, as you have learned, governments thrive on creating fear and need. No matter how well humans are getting along in their productive lives, governments will frequently and inevitably intervene to mess things up, typically with their "solutions."

Things can change quickly from times of plenty to times of uncertainty. I examine my own preparedness for change, for adapting and overcoming, and I am excited to appreciate that I am far from perfect. This time of government-caused crisis is a great time for all of us to learn, grow and thrive.

> *"How long are you going to wait before you demand the best for yourself and in no instance bypass the discriminations of reason? You have*

been given the principles that you ought to endorse, and you have endorsed them. What kind of teacher, then, are you still waiting for in order to refer your self-improvement to him? You are no longer a boy but a full-grown man. If you are careless and lazy now and keep putting things off and always deferring the day after which you will attend to yourself, you will not notice that you are making no progress but you will live and die as someone quite ordinary.

From now on, then, resolve to live as a grown-up who is making progress, and make whatever you think best a law that you never set aside. And whenever you encounter anything that is difficult or pleasurable or highly or lowly regarded, remember that the contest is now, you are at the Olympic games, you cannot wait any longer, and that your progress is wrecked or preserved by a single day and a single event. This is how Socrates fulfilled himself by attending to nothing except reason in everything he encountered. And you, although you are not yet Socrates, should live as someone who at least wants to be Socrates." – Epictetus. Discourses

Do what is necessary to be a producer, not a leech on the producers. I expect that you will do what it takes, man up, and thrive. Work hard, work smart and I promise you that in 3 years you will be absolutely amazed at what you have created!

147

About the author:

I am Shepard Humphries, entrepreneur, teacher, author and mentor. You have gotten to know me throughout this book, so I will not bore you here.

Want to know more about me? Search the interwebs or visit my website: **shepardhumphries.com**

Appendix 1

Suggested reading list

"You can make positive deposits in your own economy [Me, Inc.] every day by reading and listening to positive, life-changing content, and by associating with encouraging and hope-building people." -Zig Ziglar

Zig is talking about your Me Inc. The time and money it takes to learn the following is an investment into Me, Inc. Invest some VVs and time into making yourself better.

- "Rich Dad Poor Dad" by Robert Kiyosaki
- "Cash Flow Quadrant" by Robert Kiyosaki
- 80/20 Sales and Marketing by Perry Marshall
- "High Trust Selling" by Todd Duncan
- "The Millionaire Next Door"by Tom Stanley and Bill Danko
- "Skip College" by Connor Boyack
- "Economics In One Lesson" by Henry Hazlitt
- The Creature From Jekyll Island by G. Edward Griffin
- The Lessons of History by Will and Ariel Durant
- The Most Dangerous Superstition by Larken Rose
- Modules for Manhood series by Kenneth Royce

- ☐ If your IQ is over 90, read "Unscripted" by MJ DeMarco
- ☐ Watch some Mark Cuban and Guy Kawasaki videos on YouTube
- ☐ Watch one YouTube "Productivity Game" video each day while looking at the free pdf that is in the description until you have done them all

Most of these books can be read in less than 6 hours, so if you are not working in exchange for VVs, plan on spending four 1-hour blocks of time reading every day.

The above list is only a start. Search online for **"Shepard Humphries reading list,"** and you will find an up-to-date list of books and other sources of knowledge that I recommend.

Don't forget to check out the following link for free resources: shepardhumphries.com/harsh-resources/

Appendix 2

Good talents

This is a list of jobs, talents, and skill sets that are likely to be useful during good times and bad; it is not all-inclusive. Every human is unequal in intelligence, skills, physical ability, attitude, etc. I am not suggesting that you become an expert in all; however, if you pick a few as a hobby during good times, they could make you more marketable during bad times.

"Repair" jobs

A. Medical services
B. Appliance repairman
C. Engine tech
D. Electric motor tech
E. Automobile mechanic
F. Hair cutting
G. Welding
H. Home construction
I. Plumbing
J. Electrician
K. IT tech support
L. Gunsmithing

"Building" jobs

A. Entrepreneurs
B. Carpenters & contractors

C. Engineers

D. Metal fabrication

E. Firewood gathering

F. Protection of people and property

G. Farming, food production, food storage skills

H. Self defense & firearms training

Other

A. Purveyor of "Hope" (Minister, politician, self-help guru…)

Appendix 3

Preparing for Bad Times

This article is a summary for those interested in prepping for bad times in the US. "Prepping" is a popular term for "preparing." Examples during "good times" include making sure you have enough or your favorite gourmet creamer for tomorrow morning's coffee, locking your front door, having fuel in your car and clean clothes for tomorrow, etc.

What could cause "bad times"? An earthquake, a war, racial or religious conflicts, a tsunami, Quantitative Easing resulting in hyperinflation, government oppression, societal economic collapse due to government restrictions on productivity, uprising of a competing government or other type of gang, etc. Throughout human history, almost everyone has lived during bad times for many years of their lives. A few exceptions include most readers of this article (and other people throughout history that have also been among the wealthiest 3%) in times when wars were fought far from home.

First, a six-word summary of the most important parts of this article. Guns, ammunition, water, hygiene, skills & team.

153

As you consider what could go wrong in bad times, these are some common things that might no longer be available by traditional means:

1. Water for drinking, flushing toilets, washing dishes & clothes, and bathing
2. Electricity for powering your refrigerator, heater, air conditioner, computer, phone charger, etc.
3. Food might not be available at stores or by delivery
4. Emergency medical services might not be available; even doctor's visits might not be possible
5. Police might not be available, and even if they are, response times will be very long
6. Delivery services like Amazon to your home and even commercial deliveries to local stores might be disrupted
7. Sewage systems might stop working; consider toilets and sinks backing up
8. Cash (Federal Reserve Notes) could lose half or all of its previous perceived value

Natural "market rules" like supply & demand always exist, even absent a ruling class with a strongly controlled system. Barter will remain. What is of value in "bad times"? People throughout history have bartered the following items and services:

1. Drinkable water
2. Disposable lighters
3. Refillable lighters

4. Fuel to provide a lighter-refueling service
5. Ammunition
6. Whiskey & other alcohol
7. Hope (religious, snake oil, political, positivity books & speeches, etc.)
8. Firewood, coal etc.
9. Gas masks & filters
10. Sexual services, prostitution, stripping, etc.
11. Defensive tools including firearms, bows & arrows, knives, pepper spray etc.
12. Survival tools like wood saws, plastic tarps, etc.
13. Specialty skilled trade services like carpentry, medical, auto repair, welding, plumbing, etc.
14. Food services like planting a potato garden, baking, etc.
15. Defense services including personal and property security
16. Offensive violence, roving gang robbery services, etc.
17. Food including rice, dry beans, pasta, grains, honey, salt, canned meats, canned vegetables, tea, etc… (Know that "best by" dates mean what they say. Food does not become "bad" the next day.)
18. Batteries
19. Gold & silver, pre-64 coins
20. Soap, toilet paper, plastic trash bags, other hygiene items
21. Antibiotics like Neosporin, etc.
22. Gasoline, kerosene etc.

23. Paper, Styrofoam and plastic plates, cups, and utensils
24. Coffee, cigarettes, booze

Common causes of injury and death during bad times include:

1. Violence – robbery, assault, homicide, rape, etc.
2. Infections, disease (often due to drinking water quality)
3. Starvation
4. Dehydration
5. Temperature issues – freezing, hypothermia, heat stroke etc.

Following are 16 additional considerations you need to be prepared to face when bad times come, summarized from thousands of pages of information on the subject. They are not all-inclusive, and in many cases the primary purpose of including them here is to allow your back brain to subconsciously develop strategies and responses.

1. If you live in a cold climate and your electricity is out, your gas heating runs out, and your firewood is stolen, how will you heat your home? If your home has more than one room, which rooms are worth heating?
2. History has shown that when times are bad, human niceties, ethics and principles diminish dramatically. Burglary, robbery, gangs demanding

taxes, and other forms of theft increase. Good neighbors and friends who know you have a loaf of bread will be faced with a choice between 1) their child starving to death and 2) stealing from you, using whatever force is necessary. Consider other hungry, scared and needy animals and their natural instincts. Frequently, individuals join with others of like mind to combine efforts, and this includes gangs of robbers and rapists. As "bad times" progress, groups of 15 to 25 men, sometimes double that, frequently join together to steal while defending each other.

3. If the public water supply you have always taken for granted stops working, where will you find water? Where will everyone else in your area find it? The clean river four miles away will not stay clean for long; how will you make the water safe for drinking? How will you transport water?

4. If your toilet does not flush, how and where will males and females urinate and defecate? Will you dig a hole in the back yard with your shovel? Will you have plastic trash bags to put into a bucket, and for real luxury, will you have a seat and lid like this?

5. Historically, loners do not do as well as small groups with tight bonds, family being best. An ideal situation would be extended families with many able-bodied members living beside each other. Choose your friends wisely and rationally. Choose honest, capable, loyal, principled people with a

strong work ethic. Appreciate that you and your neighbors can still work together; however, be very careful who you trust.

6. Only you and your spouse should know what supplies you have and how much you have of each. Loose lips sink ships. Remember that hungry neighbors and friends have historically killed and robbed to feed those they love.

7. Rural homes are generally more defendable than urban or suburban neighborhoods, if there is sufficient manpower to defend them. During dangerous times, at least one person from your team needs to watch the street for approaching threats. Organization and tactical knowledge is important.

8. Societal norms and pretenses change, and humans revert to a more primitive state. This means that during bad times, many individuals and crowds will not rationally think and behave as their morals would dictate during good times. Remember, good fathers and grandfathers will do bad things to protect and feed their families. Most people will neither be as morally principled as Carl Watner nor as ruthless as Genghis Khan. Natural gender-based tendencies will return, and greater than 80% of the childcare and nurturing will be done by women. More than 80% of the door repairs, fighting and leadership will be done by men.

9. Furniture, doors, window frames and other things made of wood can be used for heat. Abandoned houses are ransacked for fuel for fires, and often

valuable metals are also scavenged to sell as scrap metal.

10. In some bad times, cars and other debris block the streets. Vehicles are rare because of a lack of fuel, and driving in one will get everyone's attention, and sometimes, bandits will employ sniper tactics. It is harder for a sniper to hit a moving person in the dark than a person standing still in the light. The best tactics for traveling include moving quickly in groups of two or three armed people, but not too closely together. Move in the shadows from positions of concealment, keeping in mind that occupied homes will defend themselves from men lurking in the shadows on their property. Make sure your team knows basic tactics.

11. On the positive side, humans are smart critters. Unless a coercive democratic social structure exists, individuals will seek what is best for themselves. Austrian Economics will prevail, and to better provide for his family, a man will build, create, invent, grow, serve and trade. If he wants to always have plenty of water, and he knows that building stoves to trade for water is worthwhile, he will use his skills and other capital to create value to exchange with others.

12. Many times, governments will take weapons away from citizens at the beginning of hard times. Some people choose to hide guns and ammunition, even though it is illegal. In most places, guns are registered, and the government will know about

those guns and require them to be turned over. Many people have to make the difficult decision of what is best for their family. Some fear possible imprisonment more than they fear the probable death of their family if really bad times arrive and they are unarmed.

13. It is wise to be a handy person with "real" skills. In good times, being a stockbroker, transgender studies professor, attorney, coder, advertising executive or many other professions can be profitable. In bad times, your family and neighbors need different skills and talents. Medical, handyman, mechanical, agricultural, and other skills and services that allow you to create and repair are of great value. If you have peroxide, tweezers and antibiotic salve, it is likely that people with bad splinters will trade a can of food for a splinter-removal treatment. Your supplies will run out or be stolen, but you will always have your practical skills.

14. Mental health can determine outcomes. A survival mindset is very important. Observing the world from a stoic perspective is of great practical and emotional value. Trust your gut; if a situation makes the hair on your neck stand up or gives you a funny feeling, trust your instincts. Do not trust mentally unstable family and group members, they can do things in anger, depression or stupidity that jeopardize everyone's safety.

15. Historically, humans have noticed that having strong and tall walls around their property is a good

way to keep people away. When the windows in your home are all broken, what will you use in terms of materials and tools to close the windows up?

16. Make yourself and your home appear to be "not worth it" in terms of being targeted. Appear poor, hungry, mean, crazy, fearful and desperate. Do not wear expensive tactical clothing and carry a fancy rifle. If your home appears wealthy—if there are bars on the windows, the sound of a generator running, and wonderful smells of food cooking—your house will be a target.

Made in the USA
Las Vegas, NV
24 January 2021